July 2011

VALLEY COTTAGE LIBRARY

110 Route 303
Valley Cottage, NY
10989

www.vclib.org

Additional Praise for
Seven Steps to Financial Freedom in Retirement

"As Hank Parrott's accountant for many years, I unequivocally trust him to provide financial planning services to our firm's valued clientele. Time and time again, not only does Hank deliver extremely well planned and executed strategies that are always tailored to each client's individual situation, he also dedicates the kind of time and attention required to ensure he reaches, or even exceeds, his client's distinct financial goals."

**—Friday Burke, Ph.D., Williams,
Williams & Williams**

"Those with IRAs can benefit from a professional like Hank Parrot who, as a member of Ed Slott's Elite IRA Advisor Group™, understands the many complexities of this investment option and can evade the many costly, though avoidable, mistakes made all too often by well-intentioned financial planners. I know Hank goes the extra mile to safeguard and service his clients, having myself witnessed his commitment to staying current on the ever-changing and notoriously confusing IRA market. He is also incredibly adept at identifying the best financial planning solutions and strategies suited for each of his client's unique needs."

**—Ed Slott, CPA, Founder of Ed Slott's IRA
Leadership Program™ and Ed Slott's
Elite IRA Advisor Group™**

"They don't come any more solid than Hank Parrott. I have had the honor of working with Hank for many years, and have always valued his high level of ethics, deep understanding of financial principals, and his genuine concern for the welfare of his clients."

—Dennis Brown, M&O Marketing

"In a society where 'buyer beware' still holds true—particularly when one's finances are at stake—Hank's thoughtful, methodical, and highly personalized approach exemplifies retirement-based financial planning at its best."

—Kathleen Calligan, CEO, Middle Tennessee Better Business Bureau, Host of the *Consumer's Edge* television program

"As an independent representative of The Estate Plan Advisor Network, the nationally recognized, leading authority on living trusts, Hank Parrott is uniquely qualified to offer his clients the most proven effective estate preservation programs available working in conjunction with an estate plan licensed attorney. Through his professional affiliation and continued education with this venerable industry organization, Hank's clients benefit from an impeccable reputation for success and vast field experience as it relates to living trusts and overall estate planning."

—Henry W. Abts III, Founder of The Estate Plan

"Hank, like me, strives to provide unsurpassed service to his clients, knowing that traditional investment methods commonly employed by financial planners are shrouded in myth—or otherwise fall short. His integrity, diligence, and commitment to securing his client's financial future is palpable, as is his dedication to applying the most proven 'intelligent investing' strategies that minimize portfolio risk and volatility, and achieve the client's goals in the shortest order possible."

—Mark E. Matson, Financial Planning Expert, Speaker, and Author

"I highly recommend the services of Hank Parrott to anyone. His knowledge of estate planning techniques and willingness to patiently shepherd each and every client through the complicated process guarantees positive results for the benefit of his clients."

—Russ Cook

Seven Steps to Financial Freedom in Retirement

Seven Steps to Financial Freedom in Retirement

Hank Parrott

WILEY

John Wiley & Sons, Inc.

Published by John Wiley & Sons, Inc., Hoboken, New Jersey.
Published simultaneously in Canada.

For general information on our other products and services or for technical support,
please contact our Customer Care Department within the United States at (800)
762-2974, outside the United States at (317) 572-3993 or fax (317) 572-4002.

Wiley also publishes its books in a variety of electronic formats. Some content that
appears in print may not be available in electronic books. For more information
about Wiley products, visit our web site at www.wiley.com.

Library of Congress Cataloging-in-Publication Data:
Parrott, Hank.
    Seven steps to financial freedom in retirement / Hank Parrott.
      p. cm.
    Includes index.
    ISBN 978-1-118-09528-7 (hardback); 978-1-118-11187-1 (ebk);
    978-1-118-11188-8 (ebk); 978-1-118-11189-5 (ebk)
      1. Retirement income. 2. Finance, Personal. 3. Estate planning.
    I. Title.
  HG179.P238 2011
  332.024'014–dc22

                        2011012857

Printed in the United States of America
10 9 8 7 6 5 4 3 2 1

To my mom: Some of my earliest and fondest memories are of sitting together with you reading. You taught me to read before I ever attended school and instilled a love of books and learning that has enriched my life beyond measure. You lived a hard and all too short life, but I see evidence of your love every day. Not a day goes by that I don't think of you and the lessons you taught me.

Contents

Introduction

Learn from the mistakes of others; you can't live long enough to make them all yourself.

—Eleanor Roosevelt

I believe there are clues in the past that can help us make more sense of our fast-moving, ever-changing, present-day world. Studying the past can also help us more effectively and realistically plan for a better future. Is it possible that some commonly held beliefs from the past that still influence how we plan today are based on paradigms that are no longer valid? Could you in fact be sabotaging your retirement and the financial future of your family by pursuing strategies based on beliefs that may no longer apply? The following anecdote illustrates this principle.

A young bride was preparing a pot roast for dinner. As her husband watched, she carefully cut the ends off the roast before putting it in the roasting pan and placing it in the oven. Her husband asked her, "Why did you cut off the ends of the roast?" She replied, "I don't know—that is the way my mother taught me." The young woman then called her mother and asked her why she always cut the ends off the roast before putting it in the roasting pan. Her mother replied, "I don't know—that is the way your grandmother taught me." The young woman then called her grandmother and asked her why she always cut the ends off the roast. Was there some special cooking secret that made for a better roast when you cut the ends off? Her grandmother replied, "No, it was because my roasting pan was too small for a full roast."

The message is that what worked in the past may not be what is best for today, because why it worked then may no longer apply today. By looking back over the last 30 years, we can see that the environment has changed. Tax rates were higher then and destined to go lower, stock market returns were higher and destined to go lower (from two decades of double-digit returns to a negative-return decade), and inflation was higher and destined to go lower. Therefore, our beliefs about tax deferral, saving, investing, income for retirement, and how we plan for and prepare for retirement have to change as well.

How we prepare financially for retirement has changed dramatically over the past 30 years. The old paradigm of retirement planning was based on the experiences of our parents and grandparents. Typically they worked for a company most of their lives and retired with a pension, Social Security, and some savings. For the most part, they were able to live on the income from their pension and Social Security. Their savings were treated as a safety net that most times was passed on to their children.

Those days are gone. Today less than 20 percent of private-sector employees are offered defined benefit plans, and the number of employers providing pensions continues to decline every year.[1] Those remaining private pension funds are woefully underfunded; there is not enough money set aside currently to pay the promised benefits to their pensioners. The Pension Benefit Guaranty Corporation (PBGC) was created under the Employee Retirement Income Security Act (ERISA) in 1974 to help protect the retirement incomes of Americans. When a company goes out of business or sheds its pension obligations through bankruptcy, it is the PBGC that takes over the remaining pension funds and pays the pensioners. Unfortunately, the PBGC does not have sufficient resources to pay the future obligations, either. According to the Brookings

---

[1]Bureau of Labor Statistics National Compensation Survey, March 2010.

Institution,[2] the PBGC has a current deficit of $33 billion, which could easily rise to $50 billion or more.

Then we have the recently disclosed vast revenue shortfalls of public pension plans and Social Security. Where will the money come from to pay these obligations? Will it mean higher taxes? Will it mean lower benefits?

In my financial practice over the past 20-plus years, I have seen countless families lose hundreds of thousands if not millions of dollars through poor planning—not through lack of effort or intelligence, just lack of knowledge, many times coupled with poor advice from well-meaning advisors who just didn't know any better themselves. I know firsthand that starting out, I was one of those well-meaning advisors. Through trial and error, I have continually looked for what really works best, for what is the truth in all the conflicting financial advice foisted upon us. In this book I share the knowledge I have gained over the years working with thousands of people—clients and advisors, those I have taught, and those I have learned from. The steps I lay out in this book have been tested, and I continue to use them with my clients and in my own life, because they work better than anything I have ever come across.

What Has Changed?

There were some critically important factors coinciding with the coming of age of the Baby Boomers (that generation born between 1946 and 1964). As a generation, a very large one, we were pretty much all in the workplace by the mid-1980s. Most of us would not have pensions (defined benefit plans) to look forward to; instead we would have 401(k)s (defined contribution plans). Our investments of choice for our retirement savings were those offered by our company's 401(k) plan. Mostly they would be stock and bond mutual funds. Our investment experience during much of our peak earning years, over the 1980s and 1990s, led us to believe that double-digit

---

[2]"The Tripling of the PBGC's Deficit: What Does It Tell Us?" by Douglas J. Elliott, fellow at the Brookings Institution, June 4, 2009.

returns in the stock market were *normal* and to be expected. This belief was further reinforced by the mutual fund industry, by the financial media, and by our investment/financial advisors. In fact, our advisors helped us save and plan for retirement based on our portfolios continuing to earn double-digit returns, with *conservative* projections of 10 to 12 percent annual returns.

How realistic has this turned out to be? Over the first decade of the 2000s the stock market, as measured by the Standard & Poor's 500 index, had a *negative* average annual return of –0.9 percent (*negative* 3.4 percent average per year after adjusting for inflation)! To put it another way, if your retirement accounts of $500,000 had been invested in the market and done as well as the S&P 500 index, the account value *after 10 years* would have fallen to $455,000. Adjusted for inflation, your accounts would be worth only $330,000! That is a loss of $170,000 of the purchasing power of your retirement nest egg over a 10-year period. Keep in mind that the S&P 500 index outperforms most actively managed mutual funds.

What if you had retired at the beginning of 2000 with that same S&P 500 index portfolio and were taking just $15,000 a year for income to support your lifestyle from your retirement accounts of $500,000? This would be only 3 percent of the account values in the first year, considered conservative and very safe; however, the effect of just trying to maintain your standard of living would have been devastating to your retirement nest egg. At the end of that first 10 years of retirement you would have only $296,698 left in your retirement accounts. If I were to further adjust the income stream and remaining balance for inflation, the actual value of the accounts would be only about $204,000! How long before you run out of money at that rate?

CBS News recently reported[3] that Baby Boomers started turning 65 January 1, 2011, and this will continue with about 10,000 Boomers turning 65 per day for the next 19 years. This is going to put a tremendous strain on an already bankrupt entitlement system, with fewer and fewer workers per retiree. Higher taxes and lower

---

[3]Sharyl Attkisson, CBS News, December 30, 2010.

benefits are most likely an unavoidable given, but will those steps be enough to solve our deficit spending and debt problems? Or will our government through the Federal Reserve continue to monetize the debt? On August 15, 1971, the United States went off the gold standard and enabled the government to print an infinite amount of dollars. As the Fed continues to increase the money supply, the specter of higher inflation looms ever larger. Will the current Fed chairman, Ben Bernanke, be able to do what the former Fed chairman, Alan Greenspan, was not able to do—raise interest rates at the precise time and in the appropriate amounts to avoid high inflation? This has proven to be extremely difficult in the past, as it has been likened to be more art than science. Will higher taxes, lower benefits, higher inflation, bigger deficits, and greater debt on local, state, and federal levels cause higher volatility in the markets? Let's not forget high unemployment and the continuing housing crisis. Would you like to know how to protect yourself against bad volatility (market values going down) and take advantage of good volatility (market values going up)?

ERISA also introduced individual retirement accounts (IRAs). This was followed by the Tax Revenue Act of 1978 in which 401(k)s and Simplified Employee Pension (SEP) plans were introduced and subsequently enacted in 1980. The passage of these acts signaled a dramatic shift in how we saved, invested, and planned for retirement. One of the major benefits touted regarding these plans was and still is tax deferral. The contributions we make into IRAs and defined contribution plans such as 401(k)s reduce our taxable income in that year and grow on a tax-deferred basis. When we retire and start taking income from our retirement accounts, this increases our taxable income in that year and we pay the tax at that time. The premise is that we reduce our taxable income during our working years when it is higher and we are in a higher tax bracket, so that when we retire and have less income we will be in a lower tax bracket when we withdraw money from those retirement accounts. Therefore, the benefit to us overall would be less tax paid and more net dollars kept.

This principle was pretty much accepted universally, with tax and financial advisors touting the benefits of deferring income taxes as long as possible, and many continue to do so today. But does this principle still hold true today?

- In the 1970s when these plans were enacted, if you were married filing jointly with a taxable income of $50,000 a year, you would have been in a 51 percent tax bracket.
- In 1980, as Boomers were starting to put money into these retirement accounts, if you were married filing jointly with taxable income of $50,000 a year, you would have been in a 49 percent tax bracket.
- In 1990 and 2000 you would have been in a 28 percent tax bracket.
- In 2011, you would be in only a 15 percent tax bracket.

We are at historically low tax rates, and when you look at what is going on in our economy, the debt we already have, the annual deficits we continue to run, and the looming financial bailouts of Social Security, private pensions, and government pensions, is there any doubt our taxes will be going up? In fact, according to the Tax Foundation of America, if we wanted to pay off the deficit from 2010 with income taxes alone, our tax brackets would have to almost triple (see Exhibit I.1).

Exhibit I.1   Federal Individual Income Tax Rates for Joint Tax Returns, Current Law versus Rates Necessary to Erase Deficit, 2010

Tax Brackets for Couples Filing Joint Returns	Current Law Tax Rates	Rates Needed to Close Deficit
0 to $17,000	10%	27.2%
$17,001 to $69,000	15%	40.8%
$69,001 to $139,350	25%	68.0%
$139,351 to $212,300	28%	76.2%
$212,301 to $379,150	33%	89.8%
$379,151 and over	35%	95.2%

Source: Internal Revenue Service and Tax Foundation of America.

Note: The rates are the same for single taxpayers, but the brackets vary. For the bottom three brackets, the threshold amounts for singles are exactly one-half what they are for couples. For the top bracket, the threshold is the same for singles as for couples. Brackets are shown for 2011.

In the 1980s and 1990s when IRAs, 401(k)s, and other defined contribution plans were being funded, tax brackets were much higher and the likelihood of lower taxes in retirement was pretty much a sure thing; therefore, tax deferral definitely made sense. However, does tax deferral still make as much sense today, when the opposite is true? Would we be better off paying taxes today when they are lower, rather than later when they will probably be higher? Taxes are on sale! Pay them while they are low! Now, keep in mind there is no one-size-fits-all plan or strategy. In fact, that is the point. Tax deferral can still be beneficial in your plan; it is just not *always* the case today, as it was 30 years ago.

Within four years of the 401(k)'s introduction in 1980, 17,303 companies offered 401(k) plans by 1984, with over 8 million participants and just under $100 billion of assets.[4] Back-to-back decades of double-digit stock market returns (never before seen in the history of the market) and the corresponding growth of the mutual fund industry (564 mutual funds in 1980 with almost $135 billion in total net assets, compared to over *8,000* mutual funds in 2000 with almost *$7 trillion* in total net assets) provided a comfort level in the stock market with Baby Boomers not seen with our parents or grandparents. It was possibly too much of a comfort level that fueled unrealistic expectations for returns and safety, which led to poor planning and set many up for heavy losses at a time when they could least afford them.

How Can This Book Help?

Chapters 1 through 5 show you how to be smarter with your money than ever before, from setting up the foundation of your financial plan to developing your personalized road map for success, strategies to maximize the income from your retirement accounts while minimizing taxes, and how to guarantee the income you

---

[4]Facts from EBRI, September 2007, and "An Update on 401(k) Plans in the United States," by John J. Lucas, Purdue University Calumet, *Journal of Business & Economics Research* 6, no. 5 (May 2008).

need while investing to stay ahead of inflation and taxes for wealth optimization.

- Chapters 1 and 2 provide the tools to measure where you are today, determine your destination, and lay out your own personalized road map for success.
- Chapter 3 is about IRA mastery: how to get the most income from your retirement accounts through a number of strategies, including how to minimize income taxes.
- Chapter 4 offers strategies to guarantee the income you need to maintain your standard of living for the rest of your life and to ensure that you never run out of money, and Chapter 5 offers strategies for wealth optimization. Let me give you an example of wealth optimization: If you had invested in an aggressive (95 percent stocks and 5 percent money market) balanced allocation portfolio strategy designed using the principles outlined in Chapter 5, starting again with $500,000 in your retirement accounts, you would have an account value of $992,806 (net of fees) after the same 10 years (2000 to 2009). This would be a total average annual return of 7.1 percent! After adjusting for inflation, your account value would still have been worth $776,484!! This is why portfolio design is so important today—much more important than in the 1980s and 1990s, when throwing darts at a listing of stocks would likely give you a higher return than most active mutual fund managers. Today we can't depend on luck or chance; we have to be smarter with our money than ever before. Past performance is no guarantee of future results.

  After putting in the effort to develop a plan and optimally structure your finances, you don't want to see all that effort go to waste through having your money taken from you.
- Chapter 6 offers strategies to protect yourself and your family from potentially devastating long-term care costs.
- Last but certainly not least are the estate-planning strategies in Chapter 7, including the five essential documents that form the foundation of a sound estate plan and how you can minimize and even eliminate state inheritance taxes and federal estate taxes.

In an *Investor's Business Daily* editorial, ranking member of the Senate Budget Committee Senator Judd Gregg cited a 1789 letter to James Madison from Thomas Jefferson: "The earth belongs to each of these generations, during its course, fully, and in their own right. The second generation receives it clear of the debts of the first. The third of the second, and so on. For if the first could charge it with a debt, then the earth would belong to the dead and not the living generation. Then no generation can contract debts greater than may be paid during the course of its own existence." Senator Gregg went on to say: "Right now we are on a perilous and unsustainable fiscal course, which, if left unchecked, will lead to some disastrous results—devaluation of the dollar, massive inflation, and a confiscatory tax rate on our children that will destroy any hope for the same economic opportunities and lifestyle that we have enjoyed."

Senator Gregg was speaking to the country, and whether or not his warning is heeded, we as individuals can act to protect our families. Through proper estate planning we can at least help insulate our children and grandchildren from the economic effects he warns of.

As You Begin

The writing is on the wall; the financial responsibility for our retirement increasingly falls on us individually. This book is about how you can minimize income taxes, replace lost benefits, protect the purchasing power of your dollars by safely staying ahead of inflation, take advantage of good volatility while avoiding bad volatility, eliminate inheritance taxes and estate taxes, and much, much, more. To do so may require a paradigm shift in some commonly held beliefs, thinking outside the box. I promise it will be worth your time and effort.

Throughout this book are tips and strategies to help you get the most return for the least risk, to protect yourself and your family, and to have your money working as hard for you as you did for it throughout your lifetime and potentially for generations to come.

Seven Steps to Financial Freedom in Retirement

1

Getting the Nest Egg Ready to Hatch

I'd like to live as a poor man with lots of money.

—Pablo Picasso

Like so many of my clients, Sharon came to me because she was worried sick about her money. A 67-year-old retiree, Sharon was so convinced she would outlast her savings that she'd begun depriving herself of the basic comforts of life, canceling her cable and turning the heat down in the winter. Most ominously, she'd started taking unnecessary risks. On the advice of her stockbroker, who was more concerned with maximizing returns than determining her real needs, she had invested in aggressive growth mutual funds to supplement what she saw as an insufficient nest egg.

While Sharon's stockbroker encouraged her to make risky investments, I took a different approach: I sat her down and comprehensively assessed every aspect of her financial situation. I looked at all her holdings—her pension, her retirement accounts, her 401(k), her Social Security—and the post-retirement income she'd been drawing from these resources. Next, we went over her monthly lifestyle expenses to determine what she needed to live comfortably through her golden years.

What I found was that Sharon's worries were largely unfounded, and that reallocating her money into a number of low-risk investments would provide a comfortable and sustained income for years to come. Had she kept her money in high-risk stocks, she likely would have lost up to half her nest egg in the recent economic collapse. Instead, I was able to all but eliminate risk from her portfolio, putting her mind at ease and allowing her to enjoy her retirement years to the fullest.

A New Approach

Sharon's story is not unusual. In fact, you might be in the same place. You've spent your entire career building your nest egg for retirement. Now you're ready for it to hatch into what you hope will be a consistent, comfortable income for the rest of your life. You may be worried that it won't be enough. You may wonder if you're being too aggressive with your money—or not aggressive enough. You may wonder if your portfolio provides enough liquidity to prepare you for an emergency. When your livelihood is at question, it's understandable to be concerned.

As my clients know, I take a comprehensive approach to financial planning that ensures that all your concerns are addressed. I begin by sitting down with you and exploring what you have—the sum total of your accounts, funds, holdings, assets, and liabilities. Then I work with you to determine your current and projected income and expenses (e.g., the monthly income, accounting for inflation and taxes, you require to live comfortably, for now and for the years to come). Finally, I work with you to develop an investment plan based on your needed rate of return, and then position your assets with the goal of minimizing risk and protecting your principal while providing sufficient growth to attain that needed rate of return.

There is an old parable I remember from grade school I sometimes use to illustrate my comprehensive approach. It is about six blind men and an elephant. The story is that a wise king asked six blind men to approach an elephant staked out in his courtyard and to then describe the elephant to the king. The first blind man approached the elephant and touched its leg, and then told the king an elephant was like a tree. The second blind man approached the elephant and touched its side, and then told the king the elephant was like a large wall. The third blind man approached the elephant and touched its tail, and then told the king the elephant was like a rope. The fourth blind man approached the elephant and touched its ear and told the king the elephant was like a large fan. The fifth blind man approached the elephant and touched its tusk and told the king the elephant was like a spear. Lastly, the sixth blind man approached the elephant and touched its trunk and told the king the elephant was like a large serpent. The blind men all argued vehemently among themselves as to the true nature of the elephant, until the wise king explained to them that there was some truth in each of their perceptions yet none had grasped the whole truth of the elephant.

Think of the elephant as a metaphor for your life, large and complex, with many moving parts. (See Exhibit 1.1.) Think of working with a different adviser for each of these parts. Each adviser would have a different perspective, yet none would see the whole picture or how important it is for the different parts to work together.

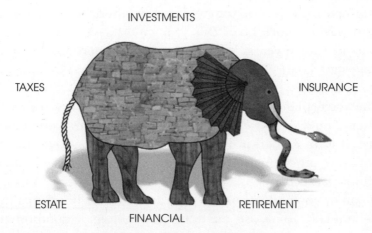

Exhibit 1.1   Blind Man's View of the Elephant

All too often, I see other financial advisers and brokers behaving very much like those blind men. Some are concerned solely with selling stocks, mutual funds, and other securities; to them, financial planning is simply a matter of putting together an optimum stock portfolio. Have you ever had the experience of going to an investment adviser who has you fill out an investment risk tolerance questionnaire? Their goal is to attain the highest return based on your tolerance for volatility within your portfolio. Do they discuss what tax bracket you are in? Tax favored portfolio design may improve your net returns, especially for those in the highest brackets. After all it is not just what you make, it's what you keep. Do they discuss your income needs, now or in retirement? This is extremely important when it comes to volatility in a portfolio as it can magnify losses and either dramatically reduces your income or the time your money will last. A comprehensive financial plan will accommodate your income needs and minimize volatility in your portfolio without sacrificing returns.

An insurance agent or adviser typically approaches planning from the perspective of minimizing risk. They may place a disproportionate emphasis on life insurance and annuities seeking the guarantees these products provide. Though these products may play an important role in a comprehensive plan they are *not* a complete solution.

Tax advisers and preparers typically seek to reduce your income taxes for the current year, when there may be instances wherein paying more taxes this year could save you much more in taxes in future years. What about state inheritance taxes and federal estate taxes? These are areas usually covered by your estate-planning attorney.

The ideal plan is one in which all your advisers are working together. Think of the elephant as a metaphor for your financial picture. If your advisers are focused on just one part—to the exclusion of your other goals—it may well have an adverse impact on your financial security.

If you're focused on one aspect and remain blind to the rest you're unlikely to devise anything resembling a comprehensive financial plan.

My approach considers the whole elephant, so to speak. While an insurance salesman might try to convince you of the virtues of annuities versus mutual funds, I have no interest in such debates. Just as the trunk is as crucial to the elephant as the tusks, annuities and mutual funds are two products that can and should play a complementary role in a complete financial plan. My process assesses where you are and where you want to be, and explores every available means to get you there.

In this chapter, I discuss the first step in the process: determining what assets you have available, where they are, and how they're working for you. Like Sharon, you may be pleasantly surprised at how easy it is to attain and maintain the lifestyle you want!

What You've Got

Your retirement resources are most likely spread over various accounts: 401(k)s, Individual Retirement Accounts (IRAs), non-retirement accounts, your home, annuities, and Certificates of Deposit (CDs), just to name a few. You probably also have, or will have, sources of retirement income such as Social Security and possibly company pension plans. In addition, you may have earned income if you continue working into your retirement years. Today more than ever, people are finding ways to supplement their retirement income, whether through part-time work, setting their own hours as consultants, or simply pursuing their passions in ways that can keep them busy and bring in a little money on the side.

Here is a laundry list of the main retirement resources you may be able to draw upon:

- IRAs—Roth, Traditional, and inherited.
- Company-sponsored 401(k) or 403(b) plans, defined benefit plans, defined contribution plans, and profit sharing plans (PSPs).
- Social Security benefits.
- Annuities.
- Other assets, including inheritances and equity and capital gains in your investment/rental properties.

- Non-qualified (not part of an IRA or company retirement plan) savings and investments such as mutual funds, stock portfolios, bonds, Exchange Traded Funds (ETFs), and real estate investment trusts (REITs), as well as non-qualified accounts for liquidity needs such as CDs, savings/checking/money market accounts, and fixed annuities.
- Life insurance.

Each of these resources has the potential to contribute to your retirement income in different ways. Investment strategies will necessarily change as you grow older, and I develop plans for and with my clients that are flexible and allow for changes as we see what life brings their way. Once you are actually retired, your focus should shift more to generating income and maintaining your financial security by protecting the resources you've built up over the years.

Let's take a quick look at each available retirement resource.

Company Retirement Plans

Many companies provide retirement plans as an employment benefit. There are two main types of company-sponsored plans: defined benefit and defined contribution.

Defined benefit plans, commonly known as **pensions**, are increasingly rare in the private sector, but still widely used for government employees. These plans provide you a specified monthly payment, the amount of which is typically based on your salary and the number of years you spent at the company or organization. You usually have the option of taking the payments over the course of your lifetime, or on a joint-life basis so your spouse can continue to get payments if you die first. The joint life option will result in a lower payout than the single life payout and if you die first, your spouse would typically get 50 percent of what you were receiving. If you wish to opt out of the joint-life provision, you will most likely have to get your spouse's (or ex-spouse's) permission in writing. You may also have the option of taking your pension as a lump sum. This has many advantages, such as putting you in control of this asset and how and where it is invested, choosing what income stream you wish to elect, and the ability to raise or lower it as needed. By rolling the lump sum into an IRA you can also control the tax consequences and thus increase the tax planning options available to you. This also allows your spouse to retain any remaining pension assets after your death and thus continue to provide for his or her income needs.

Defined Contribution plans, which include **401(k)s** and **403(b)s**, are established by your company, but rely on you to make contributions at your discretion; typically you can choose from investment options determined by your company. The money is yours, not the company's, though some employers match a percentage of your contributions to the fund. When you leave the company, you can normally take your money and any vested employer contributions with you.

Since this is your money, there are fewer restrictions on it, giving you more control. For instance:

- Your spouse (or ex-spouse) gets little or no say in how the money is paid out (although a spouse may have to provide written consent if he or she is not named the primary beneficiary in the event of your death).
- Even if you are age 59½ and have started taking income from these accounts, you have the option of stopping, making changes, or even contributing more money if you meet certain income requirements.
- It can be re-allocated in a number of ways to manage and reduce your taxes, as well as to increase your retirement income stream.
- The money can also be invested in ways that can greatly enhance the safety of your principal, as I demonstrate in later chapters.
- When you leave your employer you can transfer your plan into an IRA, which provides more investment options, greater control, and additional tax planning options.

Defined Contribution plans, including such similar plans as Simplified Employee Pension (SEP) plans, are covered in greater depth in later chapters.

Individual Retirement Accounts

Individual Retirement Accounts (IRAs) are the most common personal retirement plans, and offer far more flexibility in investment options than a 401(k). Whether you have a traditional IRA (which is tax-deferred until withdrawal), a Roth IRA (in which taxes are paid up front, allowing for tax-free growth), or some combination of the two, you are the one who controls the money. IRAs have a greater breadth of investment options than Defined Contribution plans. You may increase or decrease distributions at your discretion without penalty after age 59½ (and for traditional IRAs after age 70½) as long as you at least take any required minimum distributions. The flexibility of IRAs also allows you more tax planning options, which can reduce the tax impact of your distributions.

IRAs, the benefits of Traditional versus Roth IRAs, and related accounts such as 457 plans are discussed in greater depth in the next chapter.

Other Pension Plans

Most retirees are or will soon become eligible for Social Security or similar benefits (State, railroad, Federal, military, etc.). These plans are often adjusted for inflation, but not always as much as increases in the consumer price index. This still gives them a major advantage over defined benefit plans that, for the most part, do not adjust for inflation.

Non-Retirement Accounts

You may have a significant portion of your assets invested in non-retirement accounts. Included in this category are mutual funds, bank accounts, and annuities.

Equity Investments, such as **mutual funds**, **stock portfolios**, and **REITs** can provide a major boost to your retirement income stream. While each of these investments is taxable, those investments involving long-term taxable gains are often taxed at very favorable rates. Others, including **variable annuities**, are not taxed until you take withdrawals or surrender the contract and are then taxed at potentially higher ordinary income tax rates. This is just one reason why these may not be the best option for someone wanting to invest in the market. Variable annuities and the tax implications of all of these investments are discussed in greater depth in Chapter 4.

Fixed Investments, which include both taxable and tax-free **bonds**, can provide a valuable income stream during retirement. I often advise my clients to structure their holdings in such a way that the bonds pay income at different times and mature at regular intervals. Another form of fixed investments are **traditional annuities**, which are used by many of my clients as a safe means of supplementing their retirement savings plan with a reliable income stream. You purchase this type of annuity from an insurance company with a lump sum, and in exchange they give you income payments guaranteed for a period of years or even guaranteed for the rest of your life.

Bank Investments, such as **Certificates of Deposit (CDs)**, **checking accounts**, and **savings accounts**, tend to be both safe and liquid, providing an excellent source for money to pay your monthly retirement income expenses, for emergency funds, and for other short-term income needs. The interest earned by these investments is taxed at ordinary income tax rates. I often "ladder" CDs by spreading the money over multiple accounts to achieve sufficient liquidity and maximum interest, as I demonstrate in later chapters.

Fixed Index Annuities have been around for over 15 years, with many improvements made in these products since their inception. As with any investment it is important to compare rates, crediting strategies, surrender penalty periods, and other features. Fixed index annuities provide the safety of a fixed investment with growth linked to the stock market through an equity index. They are linked to stock indexes like the S&P 500, but also have a guaranteed minimum interest rate, so your principal is not put at risk by unexpected declines in the market. Fixed Index Annuities can also provide you with an income stream guaranteed for life. Some companies even provide this guarantee while still allowing access to the accumulated lump sum value of your annuity. I use this feature to help my clients create their own private pension plan while maintaining the flexibility of having access to the lump sum.

Life Insurance Cash Values can be a major source of retirement income and they are typically used in more advanced planning strategies—whole life policies, for example, have an investment component that can grow tax-deferred. Remember that there are many considerations when taking money out of a life insurance policy. At the same time, many life insurance policies have been set up and funded in a way that allows you to take tax-advantaged income out at retirement without reducing the face value of the policy.

All of the above non-retirement assets provide you with the opportunity to withdraw money in highly tax-advantaged ways. This flexibility is essential when you find it necessary to adjust your retirement income stream due to unforeseen changes in your needs over the years. When such adjustments become necessary, it's important to know how to reallocate them in a way that reduces the risk of losing the principal while maximizing your income stream.

Additional Sources of Retirement Income

Potential sources of retirement income are not limited to retirement plans, bank accounts, and stock holdings.

Rental and Investment Properties can be an additional source of retirement income if you have substantial equity in these homes. While you may not wish to touch this resource to gain tax-free cash, at least you have the peace of mind of knowing that there is another option available if you need it. There are people who tap their properties for equity lines of credit, take out reverse mortgages, or liquidate them altogether. Still others decide to downsize their home and take advantage of the $250,000/$500,000 (individual/couple) capital gains tax exclusion on the sale of a primary residence.

Tip

Taking advantage of the equity in your home or investment properties is generally reserved for advanced financial planning strategies, and as such should not be undertaken lightly. Always consult with a qualified financial professional before making such a decision.

Inheritances often provide a financial windfall for my clients. While it is not necessarily a good idea to plan on spending money you have not yet received, it would be similarly imprudent to ignore this potential asset when planning for retirement.

Work, as mentioned above, is increasingly popular among retirees, either to supplement income or simply as a way of being productive. Some people find ways to continue working in their field—I had one client who stayed in his job well into his 70s because it had great prescription drug benefits, and another who worked as a consultant a few days a week.

Others may choose to pursue a passion: I have another client who loves working with wood, and started a custom-made furniture and cabinet business in his home woodshop that provides him additional income while doing the work he loves. Yet another loves playing golf, and has a part-time job in the pro shop at his local golf course, where he gets paid to talk about golf all day! Another heads the music program at her local church, again doing something she loves for a cause she believes in and earning extra income in the bargain.

For that matter, a lot of retirees just like to be productive to continue to add value to our world, whether it is doing something they love, serving a cause, supporting an organization or charity they believe in, or just continuing to do something they are good at. They now have the freedom and the time to pursue these endeavors where the money is the icing on the cake.

Where Are *Your* Retirement Resources?

As the preceding lists make clear, there are many retirement resources at your disposal, and you may not be clear on how best to utilize each resource with respect to taxes and inflation. If you are already retired, you have many steps you can still take that will enhance your cash flow and (more importantly) protect the financial resources you have already established.

For this reason, I work with each new client to inventory their resources, so that they can make the most of their holdings with the least amount of risk and taxation possible. Whether you are already retired or just getting your ducks in a row, Exhibit 1.2—an excerpt of the Financial Lifestyle Questionnaire™ I fill out with each new client—will help you develop a clearer picture of your financial state.[1] (See Appendix C.)

With Assets Comes Expenses

Of course, no discussion about your money would be complete without looking at your expenses, debts, and other obligations.

Many of your daily expenses will remain the same during retirement, while other income needs are likely to go up. Keep in mind that your former employer will probably no longer pay for your health insurance and that you will likely incur Medicare costs (though everyone's insurance and health care situation is different). You may also wish to travel or pursue hobbies and other interests. At the same time, other expenses may go down—you don't have to commute to work on a daily basis, for instance.

I work with all of my clients to paint a comprehensive picture of their lifestyle expenses, for now and for the foreseeable future. Let's look at some of the obligations and expenses you'll need to consider:

- Mortgage or rent
- Strategies for reducing taxes are covered in depth throughout succeeding chapters
- Utilities, such as gas, heat, electric, water, telephone, cable, Internet, cell phone, and so on
- Insurance, such as homeowners, renter's, auto, life, medical, Long-term care, disability, liability, and so on
- Food
- Entertainment
- Vacations
- Clothes
- Emergency repairs
- Medical expenses, deductibles, co-pays, prescriptions, and so on

---

[1] To download the full Financial Lifestyle Questionnaire™, you can visit my web site at www.hankparrott.com.

Checking, Savings, Money Market, CDs, and Cash

Bank or Company	Account Type	Balance	Interest Rate	Term

Mutual Funds

Description	Number of Shares	Market Value	Original Cost	Cost Basis

Stocks/Bonds

Description	His/Her/Joint	Market Value	Original Cost Basis

Annuities

Company	Origin Date	Premium	Account Value	Surrender Value	Cost Basis

Company Retirement Plans and IRAs

Company	Account Value	Interest

Partnerships

Description	Type	Units	Value	Owner

Real Estate

Description	Market Value	Cost	Date Acquired

Exhibit 1.2 Asset Inventory

- Gifts
- Personal care—haircuts, manicures, massages, and so on
- Auto expenses, including gas, maintenance, and replacement
- Other debts, such as credit cards, loans, and so on

In addition to expenses for yourself, you may also have any number of obligations—situations where you want to provide for others. These include:

- Child or grandchild's college tuition, and other educational savings plans
- Charitable contributions to your church, synagogue, or other organizations
- Volunteer activities

Finally, we have luxuries: items that you could reduce or eliminate, but would result in a significant decrease in the "fun factor" of retirement. Examples of luxury items may include:

- Season tickets and theater subscriptions
- Sporting events
- Travel and vacations
- A second home, timeshare, or recreational vehicle

In my mind, the worst thing that could happen to my clients would be if they had to give up anything that mattered to them or made retirement enjoyable. After working hard all your life, the last thing you want to do is have a bare-bones retirement, as Sharon had been doing before she met me. In my experience, there are always ways to make the most of your available resources to maintain your desired lifestyle throughout your retirement.

I send out the Questionnaire in Appendix A to help prospective clients talk and get some clarity with thought provoking questions in preparation of our meeting. Appendix B helps clients to create a list of expenses, obligations, and luxury items. Appendix C would be completed after our first meeting as we move forward into more detailed analysis (assets, liabilities, and more detailed personal information).

I think you'll find the questionnaire to be an excellent tool for managing your money, identifying the level of income you need, and helping your financial professional, tax adviser, and legal specialist offer the most educated advice possible for your personal situation.

Looking Forward

Once you've determined what you have—your assets, liabilities, and income, which is your starting point; and have measured and identified the lifestyle you want to attain and maintain, which is your destination; then we are ready to map out the best route to get there without exposing your assets to unnecessary risk along the way. We start by determining the needed rate of return on your investments, then move on to the next step of my Smart Money Approach. In the next chapter, we start to look at ways to make your money work as hard for you as you did for it.

2

Putting Your Assets to Work for You

Money is a terrible master, but an excellent servant.

—P.T. Barnum

You work hard all your life to attain your desired lifestyle and to accumulate the assets you will need to maintain that lifestyle. Whether you are in the accumulation (working) or distribution (retirement) phase of your life, the next step in my Smart Money Approach will assure that your money is working at least as hard for you as you did for it.

As I touched on in the previous chapter, I try to bring a new approach to financial planning and to investing before and during retirement. I'll begin by discussing the old and new approaches, and why I believe my system is best for both retirees and those planning for retirement.

The Old Way: Maximizing Returns Based on Risk Tolerance

Remember Sharon from Chapter 1? Before coming to me, she visited a stockbroker who practiced the old way: He started by having her answer a risk tolerance questionnaire to gauge how much of her principal she was willing to risk losing. Every risk tolerance questionnaire is a little different, but here are a couple of the types of questions you can expect to see:

Imagine if your stock investments lost 30 percent of their total value. Would you:

A. Sell all of your shares
B. Sell some of your shares
C. Do nothing
D. Buy more shares

Consider the following statement: "I am comfortable with volatile investments that have potential for high returns, but which may also experience significant declines in value." Do you:

A. Strongly disagree
B. Disagree
C. Somewhat agree
D. Agree
E. Strongly agree

Based on her answers to this questionnaire, Sharon's stockbroker selected a suitable model portfolio for her money—one that exposed her to considerable risk. What the questionnaire failed to take into account was that Sharon's needs had changed as she'd grown older and retired. It's a lesson that all investors should learn: Because you will soon stop working full-time and accumulating assets (if you haven't already), you'll find it more difficult to offset any serious losses you may incur in the stock market. Furthermore, your approach to investing should have changed since your working years: Where before you focused on growth and wealth accumulation, today you are likely more concerned with income and wealth preservation. As you approach and enter your retirement years, you should be minimizing risk—not maximizing it based on your supposed risk tolerance.

I am not saying risk tolerance questionnaires have no value; indeed, I use my own variation of the questionnaire with clients who wish to invest their money. But taken on their own they fail to account for your overall financial picture, and as such they constitute only a small part of my approach to financial planning.

I further detail the various pros and cons to the risk tolerance approach in my chapter on investing.

The Hank Parrott Way: The Smart Money Approach

My belief is that a comprehensive and intelligent approach is critical if you want to have a stable, predictable retirement income stream. As I explain later in the book, there are ways to minimize and, in some cases, nearly eliminate your risk exposure.

For now, the most important step you can take is to get control over your retirement funds and the way they're distributed. To do this, you must work to determine your specific retirement goals and lifestyle needs, as they form the foundation of the Smart Money Approach.

Barbara was a 70-year-old retiree when she visited me shortly after her husband's death. Much like Sharon, Barbara had first visited a financial adviser who was primarily concerned with maximizing her returns—in this case, by advising her to put her money in variable annuities, despite her desire for a conservative approach that maximized liquidity. Fortunately, she opted to get a second opinion before making a decision. It turned out to be a wise choice, as investing in variable annuities would have proven disastrous in the ensuing stock market collapse (and as a retiree, she would not have time to recoup her losses).

I looked at Barbara's holdings and income needs and formulated an asset allocation strategy that provided for her needs while minimizing her risk. As she had expressed concern that her income stream would be insufficient, I took an approach that erred on the side of liquidity, allocating nearly double the usual proportions to her checking account and emergency fund. I set up an immediate annuity that provided her with the income she needed, and then laddered (spread the money over multiple annuities) a series of short- and long-term annuities that provided her with liquidity, flexibility, and earning power.

Barbara's example is typical of the asset allocation approach I take in organizing my clients' accounts. As a general rule I start by organizing your assets into suitable accounts, in appropriate amounts, to provide you with necessary liquidity and to maximize your rate of return:[1]

Operating Fund	1–3x Monthly Lifestyle Expenses	0–1% ROR
Emergency Fund	3–6x Monthly Lifestyle Expenses	1–3% ROR
Short-Term Fund	1–5 years of planned expenditures	2–4% ROR
Long-Term Fund	(Based on projected lifestyle)	5–9% ROR

The **Operating fund** is typically just your checking account. You use it to pay your daily and monthly expenses. As such it needs to be very liquid and readily available for withdrawal without penalty or restrictions.

The **Emergency Fund** is to be used for unforeseen expenses—life's little "gotchas." Money market or savings accounts generally work for this fund. They may have some restrictions as to how many transactions you can make in a month (which should not be a problem), and in exchange pay a little more interest.

As you can see, the accounts that are most readily accessible also pay the least amount of interest. The goal is therefore to strike a balance: You want to have sufficient access to funds to pay for the necessary expenses without penalties, yet not have more than is necessary (due to the opportunity cost of tying up your money in low-interest accounts).

The **Short-Term Fund** can be made up of a combination of CDs and fixed annuities, with differing maturity dates based on when you will need the money. The Short-Term Fund is for larger, foreseeable, planned expenditures outside of your regular monthly expenses. The critical difference from the emergency fund is that this is used for expenses you've planned on. If you are planning to replace your car in a few years, you use the Short-Term Fund; if your car breaks down, you use your Emergency Fund.

---

[1]This is a general outline of my system for organizing accounts; for a more comprehensive look at the funds breakdown, please visit my web site at www.hankparrott .com.

These first three funds provide you the liquidity you need while seeking to maximize interest. If you have $50,000 to $100,000 or more spread among these accounts this strategy alone could provide you with an additional $1,000 to $4,000 a year in interest.

Having taken care of your liquidity needs, the final category is your **Long-Term Fund**. This is where you invest for long-term growth, with an eye toward income for now and in the future. This category includes your retirement accounts—IRAs, 401Ks, 457s, 403Bs, SEPs—which are typically made up of equities such as stocks, stock mutual funds, ETFs, REITs, and so on. Your long-term fund may also include longer-term fixed assets such as corporate and government bonds, long-term CDs, and fixed and fixed-index annuities.

Wherever you invest, you'll likely be getting higher returns in exchange for decreased liquidity and (in most cases) increased risk. Some of these investments may impose penalties for early withdrawal, or the market may impose substantial penalties in the form of market losses. Yet some additional risk or sacrifice of liquidity may be necessary to attain and maintain your desired lifestyle (especially once you're retired).

The **Retirement Road Map** I use with my clients serves a number of purposes (see Exhibit 2.1). It is a guide to determine the balances they need to maintain in their respective funds, with a reminder of the need to stay ahead of inflation and taxes. It also illustrates the need for income from their Long-Term Fund in retirement and how that income flows to their Operating Fund for their monthly lifestyle expenses, and to replenish their Emergency Fund and Short-Term Fund as needed. I also use this in regular periodic reviews of their plan to assure the income stream is sufficient to maintain the liquid accounts, without accruing above the targeted balances. This helps assure they get the most return from their monies.

Why Do I Need Such Big Returns?

While many clients are eager to get the big returns offered by the stock market, others don't see why it's necessary to subject the assets in their Long-Term Fund to market risk in exchange for a 5 to 9 percent

Estate & Financial Strategies, Inc.
Registered Investment Advisor

ROAD MAP FOR:_____

Date: ____ / ____ / ____

			Inflation and Taxes 3–5%
Type	**Account**	**Amount**	**Est. Return on Assets**
Operating Fund	(1–3 Months of Expenses) Checking Account	_____	0–1%
Emergency Fund	(3–6 Months of Expenses) Money Market/Savings	_____	1–3%
Short-Term Fund	(1–5 years of planned expenses) Money Market/CD's/ Fixed Annuity	_____	2–4%
Long-Term Fund	(Retirement Funding) Growth & Income (IRA, 401K, 403B, Roth, Stocks, Bonds, ETF, etc.)	_____	4–9% Income

Lifestyle Expense Sheet Total

Monthly Expenses: [   ]

Exhibit 2.1 Retirement Road Map

rate of return. While I discuss the necessity of long-term investments in the investment chapter, for now I'll say that the primary purpose of the Long-Term Fund is to outpace inflation. Inflation is the silent killer of your financial health, and over the last 40 years the average rate of inflation is 4.6 percent!

To put this in context, if you need $50,000 from your investments to support your lifestyle today, in 10 years you will need almost $80,000 from your investments to support that same lifestyle. Therefore, if your goal is to live on the fruit of the tree—that is to live on the earnings without touching the principal—you would need to earn at least enough to stay ahead of inflation. You also need to account for tax rates (which are likely to rise in the near future). From this it becomes clear that, if you need a 3 percent distribution rate for your income needs, you'll require a 7 to 9 percent rate of return simply to maintain your present lifestyle without spending down your principal. Even if we were to use the more optimistic historical average of inflation over the past 20 years—2.8 percent—you would still need a return of 6 to 7 percent to preserve your lifestyle.

Of course, some don't see the need to maintain their lifestyle or preserve their principal—perhaps they intend to scale down their lifestyle as they grow older, or perhaps they have no heirs and intend to spend all of their assets before they die. In this case, the mix of assets in your Long-Term Fund would be adjusted accordingly. Every client has different needs and desires, and that's why the Smart Money Approach strives to determine their needed rate of return before putting together the appropriate asset allocation mix for your investment plan.

Checking In

The Smart Money Approach does not end with the initial asset allocation. As with all of my clients, I met with Barbara on a quarterly basis during the first year to review the effectiveness of our plan. This starts with how well the balances in her liquid accounts—her Operating Fund, her Emergency Fund, and her Short-Term Fund— were holding up. I liken this to checking the gas gauge on your car: If any of these funds have dropped below the guidelines I outlined above, we may need to increase the income stream from the Long-Term Fund. On the other hand, if any of these accounts have grown beyond what is needed for liquidity purposes, we can siphon some off into the next higher-interest-bearing fund.

Having said that, I rarely find it necessary to make such adjustments during the first year, as I will initially err on the side of extra liquidity. As some expenses will come up on a sporadic basis throughout the year, I would rather have too much cash available and not need it, than need it and not have it. However, by the end of the year it should become apparent whether or not any adjustments are needed. At our annual review, I showed Barbara that the amount of money in her liquid accounts had grown considerably since we first met—a sure sign that we could afford to allocate more of these liquid assets to accounts that would provide her with more growth. Now sufficiently comfortable that her liquidity needs were being met, she saw the benefit of transferring some of her Short-Term Fund into her Long-Term Fund. For her, this meant utilizing annuities to maximize return while minimizing the risk to her principal. The annuities provided tax-deferred growth and income guarantees, a decision that has paid big dividends.

Barbara's case is a perfect example of the Smart Money Approach: determining asset holdings and lifestyle income needs, assessing risk tolerance, striking a balance between earnings and liquidity, and making adjustments as needed.

Organizing Your Retirement Accounts

- Are your investments generating the income you want, at a comfortable risk level?
- Do you have control over the money in your retirement accounts, or does your former employer still manage them?
- If you will have the option of a lump-sum benefit or an annuitizing pension payout, have you had a thorough analysis done to determine which is best for you?
- Are you taking advantage of all the available tax breaks?

If you have retirement accounts of any kind, these are a few of the questions you should be asking yourself. Even if you're already retired and have begun tapping into your retirement accounts, there are still plenty of ways to significantly improve your retirement plan. You may be able to stretch out your IRA by modifying your distributions, and/or convert your traditional IRA into a Roth IRA, and reduce your future income taxes—and do it all while reducing your risk exposure.

Broadly speaking, there are two types of retirement assets: those you can't control, and those you can. We'll begin by looking at the former.

Assets You Can't Manage or Control

The following assets are outside your control:

- Certain defined benefit and compensation plans once you make your selections.
- Government pension plans, including military pensions.
- Social Security—though you decide when to take distributions.

With these accounts, the money just shows up. The primary aspect you can manage is to decide prior to retirement whether to take a lump sum benefit—which I recommend, as it gives you more options going forward—or an annuitizing payout. If you choose the latter, you may also be able to include your spouse in the payout (that is, set him or her up to receive payments after your death). Even if you've already made this decision, these assets still need to be accounted for, as the income you draw from them impacts how you allocate your other assets.

Assets You Can Manage and Control

Most other retirement assets are or should be under your control.

Any money you have in an Individual Retirement Account (IRA) is completely under your control, because you decide how to invest it. If you follow my Smart Money Approach and utilize the diversification and asset allocation principles that I recommend to my clients, you will be able to attain your needed rate of return while minimizing and possibly eliminating risk.

Deferred compensation plans, including 401(k)s and 403(b)s, are under your control, although you are limited by the investment choices within your employer's plan.

However, you can gain further control in the management of these assets by rolling them into an IRA, which will give you a much wider array of investment options. Doing so requires you to transfer them from the company's retirement plan custodian to your new IRA plan custodian; this has to be done correctly to avoid any tax consequences, and I frequently assist my clients in filling out and submitting the necessary paperwork.

Accessing Assets in Retirement Accounts

When you decide to take money from your retirement accounts, a little planning goes a long way. Once you are 59½, you can take as much money as you want out of your IRAs without an early withdrawal penalty. Of course, if you have a traditional IRA you'll still have to pay income taxes on the money, and in some cases these distributions could also cause your Social Security income to be taxed. (Your Social Security income is subject to federal income tax based on whether your total income exceeds certain limits. This is known as provisional income, and we will address it in more detail in Chapter 4.) Before you do anything, I recommend that you consult your financial and tax advisers first. In later chapters we will discuss how to minimize and possibly entirely eliminate taxes on Social Security payments.

When you turn 70½ you will have to start taking Required Minimum Distributions (RMDs) from all but your Roth IRAs. There are ways to reduce the taxes you pay on these distributions, as I illustrate in Chapter 3. Not taking the money is not an option, as there is a 50 percent penalty for failing to withdraw and you still have to pay taxes.

Tip

You don't actually have to begin taking RMDs until April 1 of the year following the year in which you turn 70½. However, if you wait until that time, you will have to take two distributions that year. For this reason, I typically advise my clients to start taking distributions the year in which they turn 70½, though in some rare cases there may be tax advantages to waiting.

Converting Money from a Traditional IRA to a Roth IRA

One way to potentially reduce the taxes you will pay on your IRA distributions is to transfer the money from a traditional IRA into a Roth IRA. You would pay income taxes at the time of the Roth conversion. A particularly good time to do a Roth conversion is when the investments within your traditional IRA have come considerably down in value. For instance, over the past 10 years your investments may well be down relative to their pre-2000 highs. This would mean paying less tax at the conversion, and seeing greater tax-free growth as these accounts increase in value. Once the money is inside a Roth IRA, you never have to take it out during your lifetime, as you do not have to take required minimum distributions from a Roth. We discuss in much greater detail the benefits of a Roth IRA and the pros and cons of converting to a Roth IRA in Chapter 3.

Not everyone can set up a Roth IRA, and there are income limits for establishing and funding one. The income limit for converting from a traditional to a Roth IRA was $100,000 in 2009; this income limitation went away for conversions done in 2010 and beyond. However, there is no age limit for doing a conversion. If you are 70½ and thus have begun taking required minimum distributions from your traditional IRA, you can still convert to a Roth IRA, but you are first required to take the RMD for that year, and can only convert the remaining balance. We will deal with this in more detail in the next chapter.

As of 2010, any qualified plan (including a 401(k), 403(b), SEP-IRA, SIMPLE IRA, etc.) that allows rollovers to traditional IRAs can also be converted to Roth IRAs as long as you meet the income criterion listed above. The new job reconciliation act just signed into law in September/October 2010 allows for Roth conversions on these company plans, including 457 plans as of 2011.

Organizing Your Non-Retirement Accounts

Non-retirement accounts encompass a broad range of assets, including stocks, bonds, mutual funds, and annuities. You may also have assets including collectibles, jewelry, life insurance, and real estate. In other words, this is a category that covers anything that has value and is not inside a tax-deferred or tax-free retirement plan.

There are many tax strategies that you can apply to your accounts that will maximize your income stream, minimize your taxes, and protect your principal. Let's look at how to organize some of these non-retirement accounts.

- *Stock Mutual Funds:* During your accumulation years, the majority of the assets in your mutual funds were probably allocated to equity-based funds. In retirement, it's probably time to transition into more fixed-based funds. This is the time to look at the asset allocation you need to generate the required income to maintain a comfortable standard of living. Many people have enough assets in their accounts to provide tax-favored income for the rest of their lives. When you are retired or nearing retirement, the idea is to lower the risk to your principal, reduce volatility, and generate income. As you enter your retirement years, then, minimizing the risk associated with securities may be advisable. You should therefore consider increasing the proportion of your portfolio that is in tax-free municipal bonds, government bonds, CDs, and fixed annuities.

- *Stocks and Bonds:* The same holds true for stocks and (some) bonds: as you enter your retirement years, minimizing the risks associated with such investments may be advisable. As stated above, you should therefore consider reallocating to lower-risk account holdings. (Municipal and other bonds are covered in more detail in Chapter 4.)

- *Certificates of Deposit (CDs):* CDs are an attractive option for many retirees, especially as a place to park short-term funds—that is, money you anticipate needing any time in the next five years. If you are trying to minimize taxes while maximizing income, CDs may not be the best solution. In that case, tax-free bonds and tax-deferred annuities may make more sense.

- *Annuities:* Traditional, fixed-interest rate annuities are comparable to CDs in many ways, with the difference that Annuities are provided through insurance companies rather than banks. There are a number of different types of annuities, and we cover them in much greater detail in Chapter 4.

- *Cash-Value Life Insurance:* Many people overlook the money invested in cash-value life insurance policies. The wide variety of cash-value life insurance policies available and the myriad strategies for which they can be utilized will be addressed in the chapter on advanced planning.

- *Your Home:* For the vast majority of my clients, a home is just that—a place to live. In certain rare cases, though, your house can be an excellent income source if you choose to downsize. If you wish to do so, the IRS gave you a huge tax break in 1997: As long as you've lived in the house for at least two of the past five years, you and your spouse can take $250,000 per person, tax-free, from the sale. The equity you've earned is equal to the original purchase price of the home and its current value. The money need not go to the purchase of another home, and can be invested in such accounts as tax-free bonds or annuities. There are some other strategies for utilizing the equity in your home for future income needs, and we explore them in more detail in the advanced chapter.

Looking Forward

Now that we've discussed strategies for putting your assets to work for you in retirement, it's time to look beyond. In Chapter 3 we go into further detail on IRAs and explore how to minimize taxes on your retirement accounts.

CHAPTER 3

IRA Mastery

Thinking is one thing no one has ever been able to tax.
—Charles H. Kettering

When it comes to planning for retirement, times have changed. Prior to the baby boomer generation, people didn't have 401(k)s or retirement accounts. They worked for decades at one company, built up a pension, and then retired with income for life from their pension and Social Security checks. On top of this they were dedicated savers, putting away thousands in savings accounts that sometimes supplemented their retirement income, but mostly went to their children.

Baby boomers like me have always taken a different approach. We adopted our parents' save-first mentality, but as fixed pensions became increasingly rare in the private sector, this new generation was forced to take responsibility for their own retirement savings. Accordingly, Congress passed legislation to facilitate this shifting obligation, creating IRAs in 1974 with the Employment Retirement Income Security Act, and 401(k)s with the Revenue Act of 1978. The message from private industry and our government is clear: The responsibility for your retirement is increasingly yours and yours alone. This increased reliance on our savings also means that we're more concerned with outliving our money. We need our hard-earned nest egg to provide for our retirement years and to act as our own private pension. In the end, we still want our kids to have what is left.

Even as changing times have shifted priorities and practices through the generations, we all still have one thing in common: The last thing we want is to have Uncle Sam as our largest beneficiary.

From your first job to your treasured car, taxes are a fact of life, and retirement is no exception. In fact, the shift from defined benefit plans to defined contribution plans and IRAs has made retirement tax planning more important than ever. IRAs are not only tax-deferred, they're also the highest-taxed assets you own, since IRA distributions are taxed at your highest tax rate. That's why it's more important than ever to understand how to minimize taxes in retirement, and to find good qualified advisers to help do it.

While the tax impact on these savings vehicles can be high, that's not to say that there's nothing you can do about it. Through proper planning, the tax impact on your IRAs can be significantly reduced. Likewise, it's important to learn how to protect yourself from potential penalties and interest charges. By being aware of the tax laws and finding the right advisers, you can implement a customized plan that works to your advantage.

Let's once again examine each type of income source, and explore ways to decrease your tax bill and preserve as much of your savings as possible.

Planning for Taxes

One of the biggest potential pitfalls in retirement tax planning involves IRA distributions. As the accounts have grown, so too have the complexities in choices available to you. In formulating a distribution strategy that will benefit you and your family, it's obviously crucial to avoid those pitfalls that could result in unnecessary penalties or taxes. In fact, my clients are often surprised to learn that the biggest decisions they have to make about their retirement holdings will involve strategies for dealing with taxes.

Richard came to me last year after losing almost a quarter of his savings in the stock market. A 60-year-old small business owner approaching retirement, he wanted to reduce his risk exposure and make the most out of his remaining retirement assets. Unlike his parents, who had fixed pensions, Richard needed to create his own retirement income with his 401(k). When he left his previous employer he had rolled his 401(k) into an IRA. Given the vast range of investment options available to him through an IRA compared to the limited options available in a 401(k) and other company plans, this was a smart move. When he came to me, he had saved approximately $1 million in his IRA.

I sat down with Richard and worked through the Smart Money Approach, as outlined in the previous two chapters, to determine his income needs going forward, and estimated that he would need approximately one third of his IRA's value over the next decade. We took this first third and set up a ladder of fixed investments (CDs and fixed annuities) that would provide the income and liquidity he needed over the next 10 years while also providing sufficient growth. (Fixed investments and laddering strategies will be covered in more detail in the next chapter.) We put the next third—covering approximately years 10 to 20 of his retirement plan—into three deferred fixed-index annuities, a type of fixed investment that is linked to a stock market index. Since we didn't anticipate needing this money over the first decade, we could leave it to grow until he did need it. In case he didn't need all the money allocated for this time period, we provided the option of rolling one of the annuities into a longer-term account.

Finally, we took the remaining third of his IRA and converted it to a Roth IRA. Created in 1997 by the late Senator William Roth, the Roth IRA differs from traditional tax-deferred IRAs in that you pay taxes up front, rather than when you begin taking distributions. Our reasons for doing this conversion were twofold. First, tax rates were at an all-time low, and were/are expected to rise in the foreseeable future; by paying taxes now, we were getting a lower tax rate than we likely would when he needed to take money out in 20 years (see the sidebar "Do You Think Taxes Are Going Up? You Are Not Alone"). Secondly, paying taxes up front allowed the converted money in the Roth IRA to grow tax-free for the next two decades. Since his investments had decreased in value, we would be paying taxes at the lower rate and then realizing tax-free growth as the market rebounded and the investments increase in value.

While many tax advisers recommend deferring taxes as long as possible, today many retirees are recognizing the advantages of Roth conversions. The opportunity for tax-free growth is one that many retirees could benefit from. Indeed, I consider the Roth

---

Do You Think Taxes Are Going Up? You Are Not Alone

In an article for the Tax Foundation, William Ahern discusses the effects of continuous budget deficits and the subsequent tax increases that are necessary to close the gap between government spending and collections. He mentions that planned increases in the budget deficit will cause necessary increases in income tax rates.* Using the Tax Foundation's Microsimulation Model they were able to determine the government would have to triple every tax rate to pay the 2010 deficit.

*William Ahern, "Can Income Tax Hikes Close the Deficit?" Tax Foundation, October 22, 2009, 1–5, www.taxfoundation.org/publications/printer/25415.html.

IRA to be one of the best things to ever come out of Washington. Another benefit of Roth IRAs is that you never have to worry about taking required distributions—the money will grow tax-free and compound for as long as you live. In an article for the *Wall Street Journal* Arthur Laffer, a well-renowned economist, called Roth conversions a "no-brainer" given the likelihood of rising tax rates.[1]

As you can see, taxes aren't just a secondary concern—they're an integral part of retirement planning. The key to getting the most out of Richard's IRA was determining a strategy that minimized his tax bill and maximized his tax-free growth.

---

[1]Arthur Laffer, "Tax Hikes and the 2011 Economic Collapse: Today's corporate profits reflect an income shift into 2010. These profits will tumble next year, preceded most likely by the stock market," *Wall Street Journal* Opinion Section, http://online .wsj.com/article/SB10001424052748704113504575264513748386610.html.

Tax Deferred Is Good, but Tax-Free Is Even Better

Sometimes it's better to pay taxes now than to try to put them off, particularly if you believe your tax rates may rise in the future. The "Tax Relief, Unemployment Insurance Reauthorization and Job Creation Act of 2010" (2010 Tax Relief Act) (H.R. 4853), which was signed into law on December 17, 2010, extended the Bush tax cuts for two years—through December 31, 2012. For the cuts to continue after that, Congress will need to pass new legislation—or most everyone's tax rates will go up automatically under the sunset provisions. Obviously, it makes sense to pay your taxes now! Furthermore, if your family income is not expected to drop significantly when one spouse dies, the surviving spouse may subsequently find him or herself in a higher tax bracket.

If your income is lower in some years—for instance, you were unable to fill a rental property—you can take advantage of your temporarily lower tax bracket. In these and similar cases, you may want to take some money out of a traditional IRA (to pursue a Roth conversion) or tax-deferred annuity, since your top tax rate is lower than in normal years.

In other cases, however, tax deferrals are offset by other benefits. If you have a 401(k) with employer matching, for instance, don't spend any time worrying about future tax rates—there's free money to be had. Just look at it this way: Even if your employer only matches 50 percent of your contributions, you're still getting a 50 percent return on your money before taxes! Of course, if your employer offers a Roth 401(k) option you can have the best of both worlds.

What Makes Up a Traditional IRA?

The good news is that the government has allowed you to contribute to a retirement account and use the money that would have been paid in taxes to invest and grow. The bad news is that once you take that money out, it's taxed at the highest rate possible. When it comes to traditional IRAs, taxes can get ugly before you know what hit you.

The most common error that people I work with make is forgetting that only about 65 to 85 percent of their traditional IRAs are truly theirs, while about 15 to 35 percent belongs to Uncle Sam in the form of income taxes. When you make withdrawals during your retirement years these distributions are counted as income and are subject to income taxes. Here is an analogy my clients have found helpful.

What happens if you have a mortgage when you sell your house? That's right; you have to pay the mortgage off to the bank. To help understand the differences between IRAs and Roth IRAs, think of the traditional IRA being comparable to a house with a mortgage and the Roth as owning a house free and clear. Instead of a bank holding the mortgage on your IRA it is the IRS, and guess what? It is an adjustable rate mortgage; as taxes go up, and many experts believe they inevitably will, more of your IRA goes to the IRS and less to you and your family. For example: If you have $1,000,000 in your IRA and you are in the 35 percent tax bracket, then $350,000 of it will be paid in taxes and $650,000 of it is really yours. Let's carry this analogy a step further. What happens if you have a mortgage on your house when you pass on and it is left to your children? When they sell the house will they have to pay the mortgage off? Absolutely, and the same holds true for your IRA: the IRS gets paid. The distributions will be taxable income to them at whatever their ordinary income tax rates will be.

It gets worse: Depending on the size of your estate, a combination of state and federal income, estate and inheritance taxes could actually eat up 70 to 80 percent of the IRA. Even in death you cannot escape taxes! That's not to say that IRAs are necessarily a one-way ticket to enormous tax liability. As I show in this chapter, the actual amount you'll ultimately pay in taxes will be determined by the planning you do—or fail to do.

There are various qualified retirement plans that can be rolled over or transferred from trustee to trustee into an IRA. These IRAs may then be combined with other IRAs, with some exceptions. Given the multitude of investment options available with an IRA, such a transfer should absolutely take place. You control the money instead of your former employer. Employer-sponsored, tax-qualified retirement plans that can be transferred into an IRA include

401(k)s, 403(b)s, profit-sharing plans, SIMPLE IRAs, and Simplified Employer Pension Plan IRAs. Be aware that some of these plans may include after-tax contributions—you don't want these contributions to get taxed a second time!

Inherited IRAs

It is important to note that there are different sets of rules for Inherited Non-Spousal IRAs. First, you must begin taking Required Minimum Distributions as soon as you receive the IRA, or face a 50 percent penalty. Second, the total amount you're required to withdraw is calculated differently than if you were the original owner of the IRA. For the original owner, the withdrawals were based on a uniform lifetime distribution, meaning that at age 70½ they were required to take a minimum withdrawal from their account proportional to their remaining life expectancy. For you, where you own an inherited non-spousal IRA, your withdrawals are based on a different single lifetime distribution table, meaning you are required to take larger distributions beginning immediately. This reduces the benefit of tax deferral and has the effect of lowering the gains you receive from the account. For younger beneficiaries, this negative effect is offset by the ability to stretch those distributions over a long period of time.

These are things to consider if you're going to leave an IRA to your children. For instance, it is important to remember that your children will not only be required to take large withdrawals from their account that they would subsequently pay taxes on, they also cannot do a Roth conversion on an inherited IRA. Considering this, it might be a good idea to do a Roth conversion first before it's passed along to them. In addition to paying taxes in a lower bracket (it's likely that you'll be retired at the time, while they'll still be working), you'll also allow them to take their distributions tax-free while the Roth account continues to grow.

Contributing to an IRA

You control the amounts contributed to individual retirement plans while you are still working. Your contributions are subject to certain limits and income restrictions as noted below. It may surprise you to learn that you can still contribute to one or more types of IRAs even after you've reached age 70½.

If you have a Roth IRA, you never have to take a dime out of it during you and your spouse's lifetimes. Even better, if you continue to work after age 70½, you can still contribute to a Roth IRA as long as you have earned income. So though you are *required* to take minimum distributions from your traditional IRA after 70½ to avoid the 50 percent tax penalty, you can still put funds into your Roth IRA up to the allowable amounts. Talk about having your cake and eating it too! You can actually contribute up to $5,000 per year into a Roth IRA so long as your family's adjusted gross income does not exceed $169,000 (or $107,000 if you're not married). See Exhibit 3.1 for complete information.

Of course, if you are under age 70½ you can still contribute to a traditional IRA as long as you meet the earned income rules above. As always, this type of decision is easier to make with the help of a tax professional.

Traditional IRA Deductibility Rules				
Filing Status	Covered by Employer's Retirement Plan?	Modified AGI		Deductibility
		2010	2011	
Single	No	Any amount	Any amount	Full deduction
	Yes	$55,999 or less	$55,999 or less	Full deduction
		$56,000–$65,999	$56,000–$65,999	Partial deduction
		$66,000 or more	$66,000 or more	No deduction
Married Filing Jointly	Neither Spouse Covered	Any amount	Any amount	Full deduction
	Both Spouses Covered	$88,999 or less	$88,999 or less	Full deduction
		$89,000–$108,999	$90,000–$109,999	Partial deduction
		$109,000 or more	$110,000 or more	No deduction
	One Spouse Covered—For Covered Spouse	$88,999 or less	$89,999 or less	Full deduction
		$89,000–$108,999	$90,000–$109,999	Partial deduction
		$109,000 or more	$110,000 or more	No deduction
	One Spouse Covered—For Non-Covered Spouse	$166,999 or less	$168,999 or less	Full deduction
		$167,000–$176,999	$169,000–$178,999	Partial deduction
		$177,000 or more	$179,000 or more	No deduction

Exhibit 3.1 Traditional and Roth IRA Contribution Limits

You can still contribute to several types of IRAs if you have earned income up to age 70½ and for Roth accounts even after 70½. The tax code defines some items of earned income as:

- Wages (cash or another form) from a job.
- Net earnings from a business if self-employed.
- Payments for services performed in a sheltered workshop or work activities center.
- Royalties earned in connection with the publication of the individual's work or honoraria received for services rendered.

Traditional and Roth IRAs: Learn the Difference!

Knowing the differences between traditional IRAs and Roth IRAs can help you determine which might be best for you. Keep in mind, when it comes to planning for your retirement it is not just what benefits you today. Retirement planning is about looking to the future as the choices you make today will have a big impact on your tomorrow. Give thought to the following questions:

- How many years before you will need to take income from your IRAs?
- Do you expect to spend all or most of your IRAs in your lifetime?
- Do you expect to be in a higher or lower tax bracket in retirement?

This is just a sampling of the types of questions that will determine the best IRA for you, and lead into developing your own personalized, individual retirement plan.

One more example, and this is a tough one: How long do you expect to live? You may be surprised by the answers I get from my clients to this question. Some are very pessimistic and reply, "I will be lucky to make another 5 or 10 years," others are very optimistic and reply, "I hope to live to 100 plus," but most are just hopeful for a long active life. I then ask, "Based on your health and family history what might you expect?" Of course, we can be much more precise in planning if we know when we are leaving this world, and the financial choices we are faced with become much easier. However, in reality, we just have to make our best guess and plan to account for any number of possibilities life may bring our way as we move toward our goal.

The goal here is to open your mind to strategies that you can benefit from by knowing the rules and determining what will work best for your individual planning.

Traditional IRAs:

- Contributions are generally **pre-tax**, and grow tax-deferred until money is taken out.
- Distributions—including principal and interest—are 100 percent taxable, with the exception of any after-tax contributions.
- Distributions prior to the age of 59½ will trigger a 10 percent penalty. Some exceptions apply, including, but not limited to, the purchase of your first home (must be your primary residence) and certain education expenses.
- Distributions must be taken by April 1 of the year following the year in which you turn 70½.
- There is a 50 percent penalty if you fail to comply with the Required Minimum Distribution (RMD) rules.

Roth IRAs:

- Contributions are **after-tax** and grow tax-free.
- Distributions are then tax-free if held for five years or until you reach age 59½, whichever is **later**. You can still take out the principal amount from your Roth IRA before this time, but not the earnings on that money.[2] Otherwise, you will be paying both taxes and penalties on the earnings you take out.
- Distributions of converted amounts before they have been held for five years or until age 59½ will be subject to the

---

[2]Roth IRAs follow a "first in, first out" (FIFO) rule—when you first begin taking money out, it's considered a return on principal and is thus tax-free. This is in contrast to annuities, which are "last in, first out" (LIFO)—you must take out the (fully taxable) earnings before you can begin taking from the tax-free principal.

10 percent early distribution penalty unless a penalty exception applies.

- Distributions are **not** required during your lifetime and, if you are married and die before your spouse, the surviving spouse has the option of not taking distributions during their lifetime.

- If left to children, grandchildren, or someone other than your spouse, these heirs will be required to take minimum distributions. However, these distributions, as well as the balance of the Roth IRA, will be tax-free.

The Rules of Roth Conversions

Let's assume that you've spent the past decade, beginning in January 2001 and ending December 2009, investing your IRA funds in stocks and stock-based mutual funds. As you know now, the market downturn of the latter half of this period has likely diminished your portfolio. The S&P 500, for example, lost about 3 percent annually during this period. You might well believe that you've lost the last decade of your retirement contributions.

There is, however, a silver lining. Since the entire value of a traditional IRA is fully taxable at ordinary income rates, now might be a good time to convert to a Roth IRA and let any rebounding value grow tax-free! In addition, you can take advantage of today's low income tax rates, which are scheduled to go up in 2011 unless Congress acts. Also, the revenue-raising provision of the new health care law will establish a 3.8 percent tax on investment income. This contribution to Medicare, which comes into effect in 2013, will apply to individuals with Modified Adjusted Gross Income (MAGI) over $200,000 and to couples filing jointly over $250,000. This means that if you have any income that pushes you over the threshold you will be subjected to this additional tax on capital gains, dividends, interest payments, or annuity payouts. The benefit of converting to a Roth IRA is that though the tax payment is frontloaded, you do not end up with income that could push you over the threshold and paying taxes at the future higher rates. The expectations are that future tax rates will be significantly higher and that converting to a Roth IRA will save you in the long run.

Suppose you invested $100,000 for 10 years at a 7 percent average annual return on investment. Your current income tax rate is 33 percent and the tax rate in 10 years is 36 percent.

	Value Today	**Value in 10 Years**
Traditional IRA:	$100,000	$196,715
		− 70,817 (subtract 36% tax)
		$125,898
Roth Conversion:	$100,000	**$131,800 (no tax due)**
	− 33,000 (subtract	
	33% tax)	
		$67,000

Keep in mind that with the traditional IRA, the interest you earn on that $125,898 will continue to be taxable. By contrast, the $131,800 that you are left with after 10 years with the Roth will continue to grow tax-free indefinitely. In other words, the advantage of having a Roth IRA will only grow as time goes on!

There are requirements for converting to a Roth IRA:

- There is no income limit for converting to a Roth IRA from 2010 forward.
- For 2010, when you converted you were given the option of splitting your income gain equally over 2011 and 2012 tax years, which will spread the tax liability over multiple years. Be sure to make that election on IRS form 8606 when you file your taxes, otherwise it will be considered all taxable income in 2010.
- Qualified Accounts, such as 401(k)s and 403(b)s, can also be converted directly to a Roth IRA.
- It is not required that you convert the entire amount in your traditional IRA. You can choose to do a partial conversion— where you only convert a portion of your account—this may allow those in lower tax brackets the ability to convert their IRAs in a way that won't drive them into a higher tax bracket.

Tax Considerations When Investing IRA Assets

As with any assets, IRA assets must be invested in alignment with an overall retirement plan that determines your present and future income needs. This will then determine the return you will require to meet those needs. Once again each individual situation will vary based on lifestyle, assets, current income, expenses, and tolerance for risk. I will address specific investment strategies in later chapters. For now, let's look at the tax implications of certain investments and what, if any, implications may arise from the investment of your IRA dollars.

Tax-Free Investments

Municipal bonds may be a good choice for investing non-qualified dollars—that is, dollars that are not in IRAs or other tax-qualified (pre-tax) retirement plans. The higher your tax bracket and the amount of dollars invested, the more attraction there may be for municipal bonds.

However, due to the low returns and competing tax advantages, these would not be appropriate for your IRA dollars.

Tax-Deferred Investments

Tax-deferred investments—including certain tax-deferred bonds and fixed annuities—may or may not be appropriate for your IRA dollars. Some advisers may discourage them simply because of their tax-deferred status. This school of thought contends that these tax-deferred benefits would be reflected in a lower return.

This, however, is not always the case, and I would urge you not to get so caught up in tax implications that you fail to notice the real returns and ancillary benefits provided by some of these products. Consider, for instance, such investments as immediate annuities that could provide income guaranteed for life; or fixed-index annuities that could provide a greater return than other principal-guaranteed investment options (the only counterpart to fixed-index annuities are indexed CDs). However, I have yet to see an indexed CD that provides the same potential for return as an indexed annuity.

There are other benefits and advantages to these accounts that I discuss in greater detail in the next chapter.

Taxable Investments

Taxable investments include money market accounts, CDs, bonds, stocks, and mutual funds, exchange traded funds (ETFs), and real estate investment trusts (REITs). The most important consideration with taxable investments is minimizing risk while still achieving the desired return.

In addition, it may be possible to minimize taxes and thereby increase returns without affecting risk. This is particularly true if a significant amount of your investment dollars are non-qualified— that is, not in a tax-deferred retirement account. In this case you may want to consider tax-free options such as municipal bond funds, particularly if you've got RMDs coming in from your IRAs; this will help you control your taxable income each year to avoid getting pushed into a higher tax bracket.

On the other hand, if you've got a combination of non-qualified accounts and tax-deferred accounts, some common sense tax planning can go a long way. For instance, it makes more sense to put your non-qualified money in equities rather than fixed investments; after all, it doesn't make sense to waste the capital gains treatment of equities by putting them in tax-deferred accounts, thereby subjecting the interest to the highest income tax. Your IRA money, on the other hand, is going to be taxed at your highest tax rate anyway, so it makes sense to just put it in fixed investments. This example, as well as general tax strategies for your investment dollars, is expounded on in Chapter 5.

What About Stock-Based Investments?

In your prime earning years, you probably invested primarily in stocks or stock-based mutual funds. Now that you are at, or close to, retirement, these types of investments may have lost some of their appeal, as you are primarily concerned with protecting your principal.

When it comes to stocks, tax considerations come into play. While the capital gains tax is lower than the income tax, IRA withdrawals are still taxed at ordinary income tax rates, even if the account consists largely of stock-based investments. Thus, it's probably best to keep such investments outside your traditional IRAs when possible, where they won't be subject to income tax rates.

Income-based investments, including corporate bonds, annuities, and CDs, are generally far more suitable for retirees' IRA accounts. These investments provide more security and are taxed at the same rate as when held in non-IRA investments. Leave the municipal bonds, stocks, stock funds, and options outside of your traditional IRAs.

With that said, tax planning is not the only consideration when it comes to investment strategies. There are times when the investment value outweighs any tax consequences.

Taking Distributions from Traditional IRAs

It is very important that you understand the rules when it comes to taking distributions from your Traditional IRAs because it could be quite costly otherwise. Taking distributions too early or too late will result in penalties added to the taxes you will have to pay. There are some exceptions, which I detail here.

Required Minimum Distributions

You can always take more than the Required Minimum Distribution, but if you choose to take less, you will incur a significant (50 percent) penalty. For instance, if you were required to take a $25,000 distribution and only took $15,000, you would have to pay a 50 percent excise tax on the $10,000 difference, resulting in a tax of $5,000 and you still have to take the $10,000 out of the account and pay tax on it.

If you have already started taking distributions based on the required minimum, you can always make changes if you need more income or a lump sum, though I'd caution you to first discuss your options with your tax and financial advisers. If you find that the Required Minimum Distributions constitute more money than you need, you may want to utilize tax-advantaged investment strategies to minimize taxes on non-qualified assets. This means putting non-qualified investment dollars into tax-deferred or tax-free investments, thus reducing the impact the earnings would have on your taxable income.

While there is a certain appeal to reducing your taxes now, do not forget that the money in your IRA will ultimately be subject to income taxes. Depending on the total value of your estate and the tax laws in effect when you die, this money may also incur estate taxes.

Distributions and Social Security

The percentage of your Social Security payments that is taxable is dependent on your provisional income, which is made up of IRA distributions, municipal bond income, interest and dividends, half of your Social Security Benefits, and any earned income you might have for a married couple filing jointly. If your total provisional income is greater than $32,000, you'll have to pay tax on 50 percent of your Social Security checks, and if it exceeds $44,000, up to 85 percent of your Social Security checks are subject to the income tax. (If you're single, these thresholds drop to $25,000 and $34,000, respectively.) As such, the potential impact of your IRA distributions on your gross income should be taken into account to avoid unnecessary taxation.

Distributions between Ages 59½ and 70½

When you are between the ages of 59½ and 70½, there are several options for the money in your IRA, as well as for certain employer retirement plan accounts. You can:

- Leave the money alone.
- Continue to contribute if you are still working and meet the income and eligibility requirements.
- Take out as much or as little money as you want each year.

Of course, any money that you remove is subject to income taxes (federal, state, and local) but, unlike earned income, it is free from Social Security, Medicare, or self-employment taxes.

Early Distributions

Many younger people treat their IRA account as if it were a regular savings account, taking money out when they need a lump sum for a big purchase or for expenses when they are not working. Indeed, if you need money and you are not yet 59½, the funds in your IRA can be very tempting. My advice: Don't even think about it! The costs involved—penalties and taxes on top of your marginal income tax rate—are incredibly high. In addition, after 60 days it's impossible to put the money back in.

If you decide to take some or all of the money out of your IRA accounts before the age of 59½, it will cost about 20 to 50 percent of the full value of your account. You may be shocked, but let me explain how this is possible.

First, 10 percent of the full value is owed to the government as a penalty for early withdrawal. In addition, you owe taxes on the full value of the money you take out. To compound these taxes and penalties, the taxes are calculated at your top marginal tax bracket. Using the example of $100,000, here is what you would lose:

Annual Family Income:	**$250,000; Tax Rate 35% (Federal)**
Lump Sum Amount:	$100,000
10% Penalty:	$ 10,000
35% Tax Bracket:	$ 35,000
5% State Tax Rate:	$ 5,000
Total Taxes and Penalties:	**$ 50,000**

After seeing it on paper, you must realize that there are better ways to borrow $50,000! Again, this is not money that can be repaid. IRAs are not the same as employer-sponsored retirement plans, which often have built-in borrowing provisions. Once you take it out, the money is gone.

There are some limited exceptions to early withdrawal penalties. In addition to the exceptions listed here (including exceptions for first-time home buyers, as well as for educational expenses), there is also a way to take income from your IRA prior to age 59½ without penalty. Most notably, the IRS allows you to take "substantially equal" distributions for five years or until you turn 59½, whichever is longer. If you wish to exercise this option, I would recommend consulting a financial planner and/or another tax professional familiar with the IRS rules spelled out in Internal Revenue Code 72(t).

Other Exceptions to the 59½ Rule

There are several additional exceptions to the 10 percent early distribution penalty for distributions made prior to age 59½. Among the exceptions recognized under the Internal Revenue Code are distributions due to the following events:

- You have non-reimbursed medical expenses that exceed 7.5 percent of your adjusted gross income.
- You are disabled.
- Your distribution is not more than your qualified higher education expenses.
- You use the distributions to buy or build a first home.
- Death.

Estates and IRAs

When a spouse dies, the survivor can roll over the remainder of any IRAs into his or her IRA. While this is usually the best choice, there are exceptions. For a Roth IRA, this is a fairly straightforward decision: You want to maintain the tax-free account for as long as possible, so you should go ahead and do it. In the case of a traditional IRA, it becomes more complicated and requires proper planning, as the following examples illustrate.

Example #1: David

David's wife Aubrey dies at the age of 69. David is 67, and is the designated beneficiary of Aubrey's IRA account. David can transfer the money into an IRA in his name with no taxes or penalties. He can also name any beneficiary he chooses. Since he is over the age of 59½, there is also no penalty for taking money out of the IRA. However, if it is a traditional IRA, the distributions are taxable.

Example #2: Julie

Julie's husband Derek dies at age 57. Julie is 54 and would like to begin taking distributions from Derek's IRA. Since Julie is below the age of 59½ and is therefore ineligible to begin penalty-free IRA withdrawals, the money may be subject to taxes and penalties after the transfer into Julie's IRA. It might make more sense to leave the money in Derek's IRA account and treat it as an inherited IRA to Julie; as an inherited IRA, Julie can take distributions from the IRA without any penalty. Julie might also divide the IRA and treat the part she needs for income as an inherited IRA while the balance could be transferred into an IRA account in her name.

Example #3: Felix

After Felix's wife dies, he decides to cash out all of the money in her IRA account(s). This will trigger income taxes on the full amount but no penalties.

Passing It Along

In many cases, a portion of your IRA will remain after your death. When planning your estate, the value of your IRA requires particular attention.

Naming Beneficiaries

Whatever you do, never leave your IRA to your estate. Making your estate the beneficiary could result in your heirs having to cash out the IRA over a maximum of five years, thus losing the potential benefits of being able to stretch out the distributions over their lifetime. Make sure you have either a properly drafted IRA trust or a named beneficiary.

Proper designation of beneficiaries is extremely important, so review your IRA accounts on a regular basis to make sure your beneficiary designations are kept up to date. It's possible that you made the decision years ago, and circumstances have changed significantly in the interim. I cannot even begin to count the number of times I have met with someone who had not properly designated a beneficiary!

If you have named two or more people as primary beneficiaries and also want to name contingent beneficiaries, it is important to provide the IRA custodian with very specific instructions. Consider the following example.

Example: Mike Willis named his two sons, Mark and Matt, as the primary beneficiaries of his IRA. Mike specified that each son would get 50 percent of the IRA assets. He then designated four contingent beneficiaries: Mark's two daughters, Elsa and Eliza, and Matt's two daughters, Ellie and Elisha. Mike's intent was for the two children of each of his sons to get 25 percent of the value of his IRA account in the event that one or both of the sons died before him. As it turned out, Matt wound up passing away before his father, and upon Mike's death, the IRA custodian automatically allocated the full amount to Mark and his daughters. This effectively disinherited Matt's children.

In this case, the best solution is to have customized instructions in the form of a Retirement Asset Will. These instructions may be available from the IRA custodian, or you can consult an estate-planning attorney for assistance. While the custodian of your IRA does not have to accept these instructions, you do have the right to change custodians—after all, it is your money. Another benefit to having a financial adviser is that they can help you find a custodian who will respect your wishes.

The Benefits and Protection of an IRA Trust

There are some disadvantages to be aware of with transferring IRAs to beneficiaries. For instance, the beneficiary is obligated to make withdrawals from the IRA beginning in the year after the account owner's death or they will be subjected to large tax penalties. This can be a dilemma if the beneficiary is unaware of such rules in the case that they forget to take the distribution.

Fortunately, there are ways to preserve the value of your IRA for future generations. You can do this by setting up a trust with trustees who will act according to your wishes while meeting any IRS-mandated RMDs. You can specify who gets the money, the purposes for which the money may be used, and the amounts of the distributions. For example, you could specify that the beneficiary not be able to take withdrawals from the account until they reach a mandated age of 18. This would provide you with some insurance that they not take the money until they are mature enough to handle the responsibility. It can also prevent a beneficiary from inadvertently cashing out of an IRA and incurring a huge tax liability as a result. This is just one of the ways in which you can micro-manage how your IRA account is handled after your death. But be careful how you word this provision. RMDs must come out of the IRA to avoid the 50 percent penalty. They can then be held in the trust until age 18. That option, however, leaves the IRA distributions subject to income tax at high trust tax rates.

Looking Ahead

While one of the main selling points of IRAs is the ability to invest your money wherever you please, some people may be more wary of subjecting their savings to market risk. In the next chapter, we discuss how to protect your nest egg through the guarantees offered by CDs and Annuities.

4

Enhancing Your Retirement with Built-In Guarantees

ANNUITIES, BONDS, AND CDS

Money, says the proverb, makes money. When you have got a little, it is often easy to get more.

—Charles Dickens

I n this chapter, I discuss the role of equity-based investments and bonds in your retirement income planning process. If you've felt the effects of stock market crashes, however, you may be wary of subjecting your assets to market risk. If you need to guarantee that your retirement assets will last for your entire retirement and you have accumulated enough money that an annual return of around 3 to 6 percent is sufficient for your income needs, then annuities, CDs, and certain types of bonds may be your best option. Optimally, these can also be blended with equities to provide additional growth against inflation and a stable income stream you can count on.

Bonds: What Is Guaranteed and What Is Not

Some types of government bonds—including U.S savings bonds, short-term treasury bonds, and some general obligation municipal bonds—resemble CDs and fixed annuities insofar as they carry little to no risk or volatility. By contrast, certain corporate bonds—particularly high-yield, long-term, and/or low-rated bonds—carry as much or more volatility and risk than equities. For the purpose of this chapter let's define risk as the probability of losing the principal of your investment and volatility as the fluctuations in the stock market, bond market, or interest rates. Let's turn for a moment to Exhibit 4.1. Here you see a depiction of the Three Worlds of Investing. On the left is the Protection world and on the right is the Potential world. Investors need to seek a balance between these two worlds. (The third world is relatively new, with the first fixed indexed annuities being introduced less than 20 years ago. This third world seeks to bridge the gap between the first and second worlds in that it provides the guarantees of the first world with the higher return potential found in the third world.) They need safety for their income streams but they also need to compensate for inflation so they may need to put away some money for growth. As you can see, there needs to be a balance since having all of your money in safe resources like CDs, fixed annuities, and certain government bonds, though they provide safety, liquidity, and income, does not keep up with inflation and taxes. This would reduce the value of the purchasing power of your dollars over time. You have probably heard it said that high blood pressure is the silent killer, well when it comes to your money, inflation is that silent killer. You may not have fewer dollars over time, but those dollars will buy fewer things.

Having your money in equities and higher yielding long-term bonds provides higher returns, and historically stays ahead of inflation, thus protecting the purchasing power of your dollars. These products require a longer investment time horizon to mitigate volatility and risk of loss. Therefore, you should not have all of your assets invested in highly volatile markets. The optimum portfolio blends both strategies into an effective mix. I tell more about the third world of fixed-index CDs and annuities and how they can be blended to your overall plan later in this chapter.

High-yield low-rated corporate bonds are typically the most risky investments. They carry numerous risks, not the least of which is the possibility of the issuing company going bankrupt and defaulting on the bond. In this case, the bond is rendered worthless, and the principal is lost. Although you may receive pennies on the

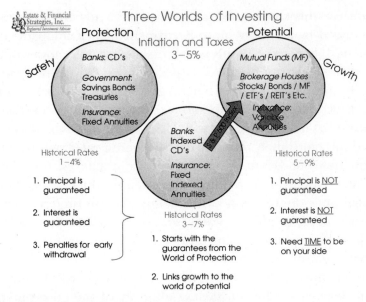

Three Worlds of Investing

Estate & Financial Strategies, Inc.
Registered Investment Advisor

Protection

Safety

Inflation and Taxes
3–5%

Banks: CD's

Government:
Savings Bonds
Treasuries

Insurance:
Fixed Annuities

Banks:
Indexed
CD's

Insurance:
Fixed
Indexed
Annuities

Potential

Mutual Funds (MF)

Brokerage Houses
:Stocks/ Bonds / MF
/ ETF's / REIT's Etc.

Insurance:
Variable
Annuities

Growth

S & P Index

Historical Rates
1–4%

1. Principal is
   guaranteed

2. Interest is
   guaranteed

3. Penalties for early
   withdrawal

Historical Rates
3–7%

1. Starts with the
   guarantees from the
   World of Protection

2. Links growth to the
   world of potential

Historical Rates
5–9%

1. Principal is NOT
   guaranteed

2. Interest is NOT
   guaranteed

3. Need TIME to be
   on your side

Exhibit 4.1   The Three Worlds of Investing

dollar on a liquidation of company assets, keep in mind that as a bondholder you are second in line to secured creditors. As we have seen recently, it can be a difficult task to judge the credit risk of corporate bonds, even for established companies. The other major risk is interest rate risk: Interest rates may rise after you purchase the bond, and you are stuck holding a bond that's making less interest than you could now be getting on the bond market. For instance, let's say you purchase a five-year bond at a 4 percent interest rate, and shortly thereafter interest rates rise to 5 percent. While you won't lose the principal if you hold onto the bond until it matures, there is still an opportunity cost: Your money is locked up in a bond that is underperforming the market, when it could have been earning more in another bond at the current rate. If you wind up needing to sell this under-performing bond, it will be at a discount, meaning you will ultimately lose some principal. The longer the term of the bond, the more interest rate risk you assume.

If it's fixed, low-risk investments you're seeking, high-yield corporate bonds probably aren't appropriate, particularly if they're long-term. For this chapter, the most relevant bonds are those that are guaranteed by an entity more permanent than a company: the government. U.S. Savings Bonds and Treasury Bills offer lower interest rates than you might get for a corporate bond, but there is virtually zero default risk (unless the federal government goes bankrupt). They are backed by the full faith and credit of the U.S. government. There is also less interest rate risk with U.S. Savings Bonds, as they can be cashed in before their maturity date if interest rates rise. Interest earned on these bonds is not subject to state or local taxes.

A related type of bond is a municipal bond, which, as its name would suggest, is offered by a municipality, often to fund a specific project such as an airport or water/sewage system. Unlike Savings Bonds and T-Bills, the full taxing authority of the government entity that issues it may not back a municipal bond. It may only be backed by the project the bonds are issued to fund. Only General Obligation bonds are backed by the full taxing authority of the government, though that's not always a completely safe bet (see the sidebar "The Risks of Municipal Bonds"). The big advantage of municipal bonds is tax-free income. Interest from most municipal bonds is exempt from federal taxes and may also be exempt from state taxes (at least in the state where they were issued).

Municipal bonds are most advantageous to investors in high tax brackets because they are tax-free (from federal taxes and some state and municipalities). As such, municipal bonds typically offer a lower rate of return than their equivalent taxable issues. Investors in higher tax brackets can take advantage of this. Let's examine a hypothetical situation that illustrates why investors in higher brackets are better off with municipal bonds while those in lower brackets may be better off with taxable bonds. Let's suppose that you have $10,000 to invest and you are thinking about a municipal bond issue that pays 5 percent interest on an annual basis. If you are in a low tax bracket of 10 percent you would alternatively only need to invest in a 5.55 percent taxable bond to match the return on the municipal bond. Alternatively if you were in a higher bracket of 35 percent you would need a 7.69 percent return on a taxable bond to match the yield you would receive on the municipal issue. This shows that investors who are in higher tax brackets benefit more from investing in municipal bonds because they would require a higher rate of return on a taxable issue to beat the tax-free rate. Keep in mind higher rates of return normally equate to higher risk.

Short-term government bonds are typically considered the safest investments, with minimal interest rate risk and minimal default risk (see the sidebar). The government has the ability to levy taxes to service the debt. The tradeoffs are that the historical rate of return may not be high enough on its own to form a strong foundation for your retirement income keeping in mind the effects of inflation and taxes. These bonds don't come with some of the guaranteed income options offered by other financial products. The best strategies will generally involve using a blend of options to attain the optimum results.

The Risks of Municipal Bonds

While municipal bonds are considered fairly safe investments, there are still risks. At the suggestion of their previous adviser, a new client once purchased municipal bonds for a construction project to build Section 8 housing in a nearby county. While it was issued by the county, its backing was based on the successful completion and subsequent renting of the housing project. When the company went bankrupt and the housing never got completed, he was left holding worthless bonds. When buying municipal bonds, make sure you know what you're getting! As a rule, General Obligation bonds are considered very safe. However, these days even some municipalities are facing serious financial challenges that call into question the safety of these bonds. In a recent *60 Minutes* report, analyst Meredith Whitney predicted 50 to 100 municipal bond defaults amounting to hundreds of billions of dollars in 2011. Though not to any specific amounts, she was supported in spirit by hedge fund manager Jim Chanos on CNBC who said "She was generally correct." Chanos went on to say, "Even Warren Buffett said 'to be long on the muni bond industry, in effect, you have to bet on a federal bailout.'" When you consider the low interest available from munis, is it worth the risk? To get higher returns requires longer durations of time—20 to 30 years; that is an awfully long time to tie up your money, especially at today's low interest rates.

Annuities: Separating Myths from Truth

An annuity is a contract with a life insurance company. There are many different kinds of annuities, providing a variety of guarantees, periods, rates of return, and investment options.

The Three Categories of Annuities

When it comes to determining which annuity is best for you know that there are three main categories of annuities.

Variable Annuities are similar to mutual funds. When you invest in a variable annuity, your money is placed in sub-accounts (selected by you and your adviser), which are like mutual funds and thus subject to the rise and fall of the market and, even more so, the underlying performance of the sub-accounts selected. If you are past the accumulation and risk-taking stage of your investment life, a variable annuity is not likely to be a suitable or desirable choice. Furthermore, the various costs associated with variable annuities can also reduce your actual return. If you're willing to assume the risk of investing in the market, it probably makes more sense just to go with a mutual fund! I talk in more detail about the importance of investment costs in Chapter 5, as well as optimum portfolio design—which is nearly impossible to attain through variable annuity sub-accounts.

Traditional (Fixed) Annuities provide a guarantee of principal, a guaranteed rate of return for a specified period, and the option for a guaranteed payment stream if you elect it. A fixed annuity typically has a guaranteed minimum interest rate so that your money will never earn less than this rate. Some fixed annuities have fluid interest rates—that is, the interest rate on your annuity can rise or fall annually on the anniversary of your policy, but can never go below the guaranteed minimum. Other fixed annuities feature multi-year guarantees, wherein you can lock in a guaranteed interest rate for period of time (i.e. 3-, 5-, 7- and 10-year maturities). Fixed annuities have good liquidity, as most allow you to withdraw up to 10 percent annually without penalty. Some even have cumulative withdrawal privileges, so if you take nothing out one year, you can withdraw 20 percent the next year. They have historically provided an average return of around 2 to 5 percent. (See Exhibit 4.1 for further reference.)

Fixed Index Annuities, also known as **Equity Indexed Annuities**, are fixed annuities that have potential earnings linked to a stock or bond index such as the S&P 500 or the Barclays Aggregate Bond Indexes. It is important to understand that you do not actually own the stocks, but that the returns are tied to the performance of the index. These unique investments offer the principal guarantees and built-in minimum rates of return of fixed annuities, while also providing the potential for higher returns based on a percentage of the gains in the index to which they are linked. You are thus able to reap some of the benefits of gains in the stock market, while protecting your principal against the risks of a catastrophic drop like we saw in 2008.

Most of these annuities limit the amount of gains you receive through provisions such as a participation rate. So if your participation rate is 50 percent, and the S&P 500 is up 22 percent, your account would increase by 11 percent (50 percent of 22 percent). While the potential gains may be less than you would get from investing directly in an index mutual fund, many of the clients I work with like the idea of protecting their principal and don't mind giving up some potential return for that protection. Indeed, there are times—usually in a bear or sideways market—that a fixed index annuity may outperform the market index to which they're linked. This is due to the fact that you are participating in the gains of the market without having to make up for the losses. Fixed index annuities have historically offered a rate of return in the 3 to 7 percent range over time, though it's important to meet with a trusted financial adviser who can help you find an annuity that offers the best rate and other features to best obtain your objectives, such as income riders; more on these in the next section on annuity payout options.

Tip: Getting Better Rates on Your Annuity

Once the initial rate guarantee has expired on an annuity, it may be worth looking at moving your balance to a new annuity contract. This makes sense as long as the surrender charges are eliminated (most annuities have a penalty if you take money out before a certain number of years have passed as with a CD). In addition, there are ways to transfer the balance to another annuity contract and continue to defer taxes (this is called a 1035 Exchange, from the section of the Internal Revenue Service (IRS) Code that allows it).

Annuity Payout Options

Since most retirees are looking for ways to boost their income, the income stream created by an annuity can be a very useful planning tool. There are various options for receiving income from your annuities. We'll start with payout options for annuitization. While you're trading in your lump sum, the upside is that you can potentially create an income stream you can't outlive—essentially a private pension.

The simplest is a **Life Annuity**. The insurance company agrees to pay a fixed amount to you for the rest of your life. This amount is based on your age, life expectancy, and the value of your annuity when payments start. When you die, any remaining value goes to the insurance company. Of course, if you wind up living beyond your life expectancy, you'll reap benefits well above the money you invested. In this sense, an annuity can be seen as an insurance policy against outliving your money. Typically I don't recommend these to my clients unless they don't have any heirs and simply want to get the most of their money while they're alive (or if they've already taken care of their heirs elsewhere in their estate plan). This option typically offers the largest payouts.

If you don't like the idea of the insurance company collecting the remaining value of your annuity in the event of your untimely death, you may opt for a **Life Annuity with Period Certain.** This is much like a Life Annuity, except that if you die before a certain number of years have elapsed (usually 5, 10, 15, or 20 years), the insurance company will continue to pay your beneficiaries for the remainder of that time period.

Related to this are **Period Certain** annuities, wherein the insurance company will make payments to you and then to your beneficiaries for a certain time period (usually 10, 15, or 20 years). Because the insurance company knows exactly how long they'll be making payments (that is, they don't have to worry about you living beyond your life expectancy and costing them money), you can typically get higher monthly payments than you would on a Life Annuity with Period Certain. Immediate or deferred annuities can be used with Period Certain payouts to create a laddering strategy for flexibility in providing guaranteed income streams.

There are also **Joint and Survivor** annuity payments, in which the insurance company agrees to pay a certain amount to you and another person (usually your spouse) for as long as either of you lives. This can also be paired with a Period Certain provision, resulting in a Joint Life with Period Certain.

The size of your monthly payments largely depends on the risk to the insurance company. For instance, a Life Annuity will typically pay more in monthly payments than a Life Annuity with Period Certain. Think about it—with a Life Annuity, there's always the chance that the owner will die early and the insurance company will be able to keep the remaining money. With the Period Certain, they're on the hook for at least the agreed-upon time period. It is a good idea to shop around, as annuities with the same provision can still vary in rates just as different banks will offer different rates on similar CDs.

These payout options all involve annuitization—swapping out your lump sum for an assured income stream. It is also possible to get income from your annuity while retaining your lump sum, as annuities typically allow you to withdraw up to 10 percent on an annual basis. If you choose to take this amount as a regular monthly income stream, it is known as taking **systematic withdrawals**. Unlike (some) annuitization options, systematic withdrawals do not guarantee income for life—you can only take out as much money as you have in the annuity. The upshot of this option is that the remaining value will continue to earn interest at a higher rate than in an annuitization payout, while also retaining access to the principal and interest less the withdrawals.

Another way you can protect your principal while taking income is through **income riders**, which have long been a feature of variable annuities but were only recently introduced for fixed index annuities. An income rider limits you to taking a lifetime income stream as with the annuitization options, but allows those income payments to be based on a guaranteed higher rate of return. Exhibit 4.2 shows an example of how Fixed Index Annuities with an income rider might work. Keeping in mind that the benefits can vary from company to company and product to product, it is important to understand the specifics of the annuity you are considering to assure it meets your needs.

Let's say you put $100,000 in a deferred fixed index annuity with a 6 percent return and an 8 percent income rider. After nine years at 6 percent, you'll have $170,000 that you can take as a lump sum. If you wish, though, you can instead take a lifetime income stream based on what your principal would have earned at 8 percent—in this case, a total value of around $200,000. The actual size of the income payments is determined by the distribution rate based on your age (see the chart on the next page). It is a guaranteed

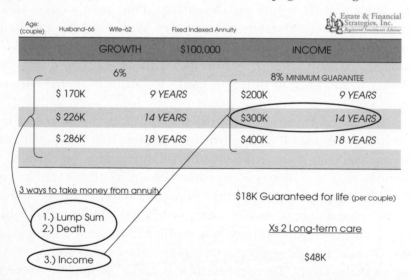

Exhibit 4.2   Fixed Indexed Annuity with an Optional Income Rider

lifetime payout (with a joint life option for married couples) while this income rider option still allows you and your heirs access to the balance in your annuity.

For example: If you invested at age 66 you would be 75 after nine years and the distribution rate would be 6 percent for a single life or 5.5 percent for a joint life. Based on this, a single individual could receive a guaranteed income stream of $12,000 a year for life (or a joint couple could receive $11,000).

How are Lifetime Income Withdrawal amounts determined? Following is an example of those used to calculate the guaranteed income stream from an optional income rider, if elected:

Attained Age (on the first day of the initial income period)	Maximum Annual Withdrawal Percentage (Single Life)	Maximum Annual Withdrawal Percentage (Joint Life)
50–54	3.5%	3.0%
55–59	4.0%	3.5%
60–64	4.5%	4.0%
65–69	5.0%	4.5%
70–74	5.5%	5.0%
75–79	6.0%	5.5%
80–84	6.5%	6.0%
85–89	7.0%	6.5%
90+	7.5%	7.0%

Another advantage of income riders is the ability to defer withdrawals and let the income streams accumulate in value. Much like deferring Social Security benefits, the longer you defer the income streams the larger they become. So in the previous example, where the individual took out a guaranteed income stream of $12,000 ($11,000 for the joint account), they could defer taking the payments for 14 years (when they are age 80). This would mean the income distributions would be based on $300,000 notional principal. Now if they wanted to take an income stream they would be guaranteed $18,000 for life! The advantage that income riders have over Social Security benefits is that you can defer a portion of the income distributions. You are not locked in for life at a lower rate.

Annuities and Taxes

One of the benefits of an annuity is the ability to accumulate money that grows on a tax-deferred basis, similar to a traditional IRA. (Indeed, many people buy annuities solely for their tax-deferral benefits.) For non-retirement plan annuities, the money you put in has already been taxed, but the increase in value is not taxed until you take the money out. Any gains or income you receive beyond your initial investment are taxed at the ordinary income tax rate—this is, it should be noted, higher than the capital gains tax rate and therefore a consideration when used in an overall investment plan. When properly implemented annuities can help you reduce your taxable income while they are growing in deferral *and* help you reduce your taxes while taking withdrawals. (I'll discuss this more in "Annuities and Social Security" later in this chapter.)

There are five scenarios for taxes on annuity payments:

Annuitizing a Contract   Under this scenario, you direct the insurance company to start making payments to you on a monthly, quarterly, or annual basis as a supplement to your retirement income. The payments are taxed proportionately—the portion of each payment that is considered a return of your after-tax contribution is tax-free, while the portion that is considered the earnings on your investment is taxed as ordinary income.

Here's an example. Martha Jennings contributed $100,000 to a deferred annuity, which is now worth $200,000. Since there is a 10 percent penalty on early withdrawals before the age of 59½, she decides to retire at age 60 and annuitize the contract. The insurance company says it will pay her $800 a month for the rest of her life. She will be taxed on $466 of each payment (the interest portion) and the remaining $334 is not taxed as it counts as a return of principal. Note that if Martha dies the day after annuitizing the contract, the remaining value of the annuity goes to the insurance company, not her heirs. This option may be appealing to those without heirs, or those who are using some portion of their assets and seeking the highest available income payment.

Following is a list of payment options seen in annuities. Some companies may not provide all these options and some companies may have additional options, but these are the most commonly used:

Standard Annuity Options:

Option A—Guaranteed period. The company pays equal install-ments for a guaranteed period. At the end of the guaran-teed period, installments terminate. The guaranteed period must be at least five years and no more than 30 years. I use this option many times for income planning. Many times I will put together annuities with different payout terms of increasing income streams to accommodate increasing income needs due to inflation.

Option B—Life. The company pays equal installments as long as the annuitant is living. When the annuitant dies, install-ments terminate. This would be most beneficial to someone seeking to maximize the annuity payout for their lifetime, without a need to account for beneficiaries.

Option C—Life with a guaranteed period. The company pays equal installments as long as the annuitant is living. If the annuitant dies before the end of the guaranteed period, installments continue until the end of the guaranteed period. The guaranteed period must be 5, 10, 15, 20, 25, or 30 years. This option is when there is a need to account for beneficiaries if the annuitant died early.

Option D—Interest only. The company pays installments of the interest earned on the Accumulation Value for a designated period of at least 5 years. The Accumulation Value will not increase during the designated period. At the end of the designated period you may take the Accumulation Value in a single payment, or you may select another annuity option. Any time before the end of the designated period, you may select a Standard Annuity Option. I have never used this option, though it could be beneficial for meeting temporary income needs while leaving your options open for a later date.

Option E—Selected amount. The company pays equal installments of a selected amount. When we have paid the entire
Accumulation Value and accumulated interest, installments
terminate. The installments must extend for a period of at
least 10 years and no more than 30 years. The guaranteed
interest rate for Option E is the Minimum Annual Annuity
Payment Rate. I have never used this option either, though
it may be beneficial for someone needing a specified
amount of income for as long as the annuity lasts.

Option F—Joint and Survivor Life. You must name two annuitants for this annuity option. The company pays installments
as long as either annuitant is living. When both annuitants
are dead, installments terminate. This works the same as Life,
but for a couple.

Withdrawals from an Annuity Contract As stated above, many
annuity contracts allow the owner to withdraw some amount of
money each year—normally 10 percent of either the original premium or the current value. This allows the owner to have access
to some of the money without penalty and without annuitizing the
contract.

There are potential tax consequences to this approach,
however.

If you choose to take a withdrawal from an annuity (assuming
you're past age 59½, to avoid the 10 percent federal early withdrawal penalty), earnings are required to come out first. These are
fully taxable at ordinary income tax rates.

Surrendering an Annuity Contract Annuities are a type of retirement account, much like a 401(k) or IRA. So while sometimes
people want to take the money and run, this can be an expensive
proposition.

With 401(k)s and IRAs, early withdrawals (those taken before
age 59½) are fully taxable, and there is a 10 percent penalty on *all*
the money withdrawn, both principal and interest. Even non-IRA
annuities are considered retirement plans (and thus subject to
the same 10 percent early withdrawal penalty) but there is one big

difference: Since the monies contributed have already been taxed, the 10 percent penalty only applies to the earnings. In addition, there may be surrender charges that you have to pay to the insurance company if you terminate the contract before the term expires.

Dying with an Accumulation Phase Annuity Contract in Place If you die with an annuity still in deferral (you have not elected for an annuitization option), the money will go directly to your named beneficiaries (who will owe income taxes on the earnings). If you have elected an annuitization option on the annuity and it is already in payout, then its status depends on what payout option you've chosen. For instance, if you chose any kind of Period Certain option, the annuity will continue to pay out to your heirs for the duration of that period. (They will likewise pay taxes on the earnings.) Most annuities will also allow you to choose a Period Certain payout to your named beneficiaries, even though the annuity may still be in deferral at your passing. This can be a great strategy for providing an income stream much like a private pension for your beneficiaries, as opposed to a lump sum payment that they might not be capable of managing.

For example: I have seen the example of a client who came looking to pass on an annuity to his two sons. He recognized though that neither of his sons was particularly good with money (they did not have a retirement account and likely never would he told me). Since he did not trust his sons with a lump payment that they would likely throw away, he invested in an annuity that would grow in deferral until the sons turned aged 65—at which point it would pay off an income stream for 15 years, effectively creating a pension plan for his children. This is just one of the many ways annuities can be customized to suit your needs.

Immediate Annuities The same rules apply: If you have a life-only immediate annuity, its payments will cease upon your death. If you elected for a Period Certain, your heirs will continue to receive payments for the duration. The payments from an immediate annuity funded with non-qualified money (not part of a qualified retirement plan) mostly constitute a return of principal, though the interest portion is still taxable. However, if the annuity is a traditional IRA, these payments will be fully taxable for both interest and principal.

Example: Laddering Different Types of Annuities I had a client, Brenda, who wanted guaranteed income for life and hoped to get some growth to help keep pace with taxes and inflation. After showing her the different options available she elected to go with an annuity ladder to ensure that she would also have a degree of liquidity in case her income needs changed.

We started out by opening up an immediate annuity that would provide her income payments for the next five years. At the same time, we also opened a deferred fixed annuity that would grow without taking income over the same five-year period. If her income needs changed over time and she needed more income than the immediate annuity was providing, she could withdraw up to 10 percent from the deferred annuity to supplement her income stream; otherwise, we would just wait five years and then annuitize it (start taking income) for years 5 to 10 of the plan. Finally, I set up a deferred fixed annuity that would grow without taking income for the first 10 years, and which would grow to all the money she'd spent over the first decade of the plan—this gave us 20 years to grow the balance of her portfolio and opened up numerous investment options to ensure she would never outlive her money. In so doing, I was able to set up a guaranteed income stream for much of Brenda's retirement. Laddering annuities in this manner provided a hedge against rising inflation or interest rates, since we did not annuitize (start taking income) all at once. We staggered the annuities by taking some income right away, while deferring the rest until the fifth and tenth years, thereby providing income and growth.

Annuities and Social Security

As I outlined in Chapter 3, your Social Security benefits could be subjected to income taxes depending on your provisional income. For instance, if you have income from other investments such as CDs, mutual funds, or distributions from IRAs, you could wind up paying income tax on as much as 50 to 85 percent of your Social Security benefits.

Annuities can help in this regard. You can move some of the money that's coming from these taxable investments into a tax-deferred annuity, thereby reducing your provisional income to the point that taxes on your Social Security benefits could be eliminated altogether. Since the earnings from annuities are tax-deferred, the income does not count for purposes of calculating the tax on your Social Security benefits as long as you leave the money in the annuities. In fact, we were able to do exactly this with Brenda, getting her provisional income below the minimum threshold for Social Security taxation, while still providing the income she needed to maintain her lifestyle.

There's another potential benefit to annuities vis-à-vis Social Security. If the amount of income you require to maintain your lifestyle is high enough to trigger Social Security taxation, we can set up an immediate annuity. The payments will come largely from the (nontaxable) principal, thus giving you the income you need while minimizing taxes and possibly eliminating your liability to income taxes on Social Security.

The Social Security Administration has a list of requirements that determines how much of your Social Security benefits you pay in taxes, depending upon your income. The list is:

- File a federal tax return as an individual and your provisional income[1] is
  - Between $25,000 and $34,000, you may have to pay income tax on up to 50 percent of your benefits.
  - More than $34,000, up to 85 percent of your benefits may be taxable.
- File a joint return, and you and your spouse have provisional income that is
  - Between $32,000 and $44,000, you may have to pay income tax on up to 50 percent of your benefits.
  - More than $44,000, up to 85 percent of your benefits may be taxable.

---

[1]Provisional income is defined as half your Social Security income plus wages, earnings, IRA distributions, interest, dividends, capital gains, and municipal bond income.

This means that anywhere from 50 to 85 percent of your Social Security benefits can be subject to taxes! However, prudent planning with annuities may help you limit your tax liability.

To illustrate this point let's imagine a hypothetical scenario where split annuities may be employed successfully. Steve and Martha are married and their provisional income is $42,000 a year. They have a $100,000 CD earning 4 percent interest. Under current law, married couples must pay taxes on their Social Security benefits up to 85 percent if their joint provisional income is above $44,000 a year, even if they do not take any of the $4,000 of earned interest and just leave it in the CD. The interest is still taxable and therefore will push their provisional income to $46,000 causing them to pay taxes on 85 percent of their Social Security benefits. This additional tax could have been completely avoided by investing their $100,000 into a single premium tax deferred fixed annuity.

Let's look at another example. In this example Steve and Martha need the income from their $100,000 to support their lifestyle. We will use the same 4 percent rate of interest providing them with $4,000 of interest, and again this will push up their provisional income, causing them to pay tax on 85 percent of their Social Security income. By the way, this applies to their gross Social Security income, including any deductions for Medicare Part B or D.

This additional tax too could be avoided, through a strategy I have used numerous times with my clients. We purchase an immediate annuity for $34,828 to provide the $4,000 annual income needed ($334 per month) paid out over 10 years for a total payout of $40,000. Because this payout reflects a return of principal for the most part and only $5,172 of interest, the taxable part of the income is only about $517 per year for the 10 years, which would keep your provisional income under $44,000 and thus avoid paying tax on 85 percent of your Social Security benefits. Now I know what you are thinking, how do you replace the $34,828 spent to purchase the immediate annuity? I am glad you asked.

Steve and Martha now take the balance of $65,172 ($100,000–$34,828) and purchase either a tax-deferred single-premium fixed annuity or possibly fixed index annuity. This annuity would then be customized to grow to $100,000 over the same 10-year period.

So now, between the two annuities, Steve and Martha locked in the income they need in the short-term with the immediate annuity, they have stayed at the lower tax margin, and they have managed to secure the same $100,000 that would otherwise have counted against their income limits in a CD. They have effectively employed a series of annuities to accomplish all of their goals.

A couple of caveats: First, the rates I am using are based on historical returns and can vary dramatically, from the double digit interest rates available on CDs and fixed annuities in the 1970s and 1980s to interest rates of 4 to 6 percent in the 1990s, with an exceptional amount of volatility since 2000. Interest rates have fluctuated from less than ½ percent in 2010 to as high as 6 percent in 2000! Therefore, though this strategy should work in most interest rate environments (as CD rates and fixed annuity rates tend to correlate), the actual income streams and interest rates can differ dramatically from the given examples. Second, in using fixed index annuities there may not be a guaranteed interest rate over the term. Historically, fixed index annuities have outperformed fixed annuities, though, as with every comparison of historical statistics, there are exceptions.

One last caveat that you will hear quite often in any discussions of statistical returns: "Historical returns are no guarantee of future results."

Utilizing Annuities for Long-Term Care Planning

Annuities can help pay for your long-term care and nursing home needs in three ways. First, they can provide the means (through withdrawals or annuitization) to pay the premiums of a long-term care insurance (LTCI) policy. Next, the income (or withdrawals) can be used to pay the actual expenses of long-term care (LTC).

There are also types of annuities that have riders that specifically provide LTC benefits—for instance, the size of your income payments may be doubled if you end up in a nursing home.

Finally, annuities can be used in Medicaid (the government health program) spend-down planning so you can protect some of your assets for your spouse. If you have money from CDs or other investments and later need to enter a nursing home, you may be able to transfer some of those assets into an annuity based on Medicaid spend-down rules to provide income for your spouse. Note that Medicaid is largely controlled and managed by the states, and there are strict legal limitations for a Medicaid spend-down of your assets. As always, consult a qualified estate-planning and elder law attorney when planning for long-term care considerations, as this is a complicated area of tax law. Ask how you can provide income for the spouse at home using annuities, as opposed to the money being required to pay for the nursing home costs. Not all annuities qualify so be sure you are dealing with knowledgeable advisers!

Charges: How Much Do They Matter?

Oftentimes clients come into my office and ask about the charges associated with annuities. They mention how they've heard about annuities but their source (friend, financial newsletter, and so on) warned them about the costs associated with these products. It is important to know that charges and fees are only relevant to variable annuities. This is due to the fact that you are charged a fee no matter the performance of the index the annuity is linked to. So you may be charged a fee no matter how the index performed. You are guaranteed very little security with these types of investments. With fixed annuities, on the other hand, you are guaranteed a fixed return much like a CD. The fees are implicit in the interest, so you don't have to worry about them.

When comparing variable annuities and CDs, the important thing to consider is the overall net return. An annuity may have more explicit charges associated with it, but it may also offer a higher interest rate that more than offsets any potential charges. Furthermore, if the features offered by the annuity are important to you, any associated charges may be worth it.

Annuities are like any investment—you need to sit down with your adviser, determine what kind of return you'll need, when you'll need the income, and what other features you feel will best serve your retirement needs. Rather than get caught up in trying to figure out what insurance companies' fees and expenses are relative to those attached to CDs by banks, you should instead consider what overall features and benefits within the respective products work best for you. Charges are important with variable annuities but in fixed annuities they are part of the implicit cost of the annuity. The important point to understand here is that you are not expected to be able to understand, manage, and purchase annuity products on your own. When dealing with annuities it is always prudent to contact a trusted adviser—there is no exception. Like any other investment, annuities should fit the context of your investment profile. A financial adviser should be consulted because there are many different types of annuities that vary between companies. An adviser will be able to help you shop around and find the products that best suit your needs.

CDs: A Key Element in an Income-Generating Retirement Portfolio

Some of you might remember the sky-high interest rates offered by Certificates of Deposit (CDs) in the 1980s—sometimes as high as 16 percent for certain long-term CDs! Of course, mortgage rates hit 21 percent at the same time, and inflation was galloping. If you were one of the lucky ones who locked in long-term CDs (or bonds) at that time, you did very well, as interest rates and inflation fell and the stock market began to recover (unless you owned callable CDs or bonds, which we'll discuss shortly). While CDs no longer offer 16 percent interest rates, they can still play an important role in the income-oriented investor's portfolio by reducing risk and volatility and providing liquidity for the foundation of your financial plan.

Of course, that's not to say that CDs are entirely without risks—call risk, interest penalties, and rate risk can come into play with CDs. In this section we'll look at some of the risks inherent to CDs, and explore some particular varieties of CDs.

Callable CDs

Callable CDs offer higher interest rates than their peers, with the caveat that they can be "called" (forcibly redeemed) by the bank or issuer under certain conditions. If interest rates are trending downward you can almost be assured that your CD will be called, as the bank won't wish to continue paying a high interest rate when better rates are now available to them. On the other hand, if interest rates rise you'll probably be locked into a rate that's below what everyone else is getting (unless you're willing to forfeit several months of interest to get out early). Since these CDs also tend to have long maturities—usually five years or more—this call risk can cost you considerable future income. Thus, I do not typically recommend callable CDs as an investment product. I believe they are very risky and unsuitable to most investment profiles.

If someone recommends a callable CD you should be very wary. Here are a number of questions you should ask them:

- **Who is the issuer of the CD?** You should know the firm that is offering this product.
- **What is the maturity date of the CD?** Be extra careful! Do not confuse the maturity date of the CD with the call date. This is an all-too-common mistake. The maturity date is when *you* have the right to withdraw all your money without penalty. The call date is when the issuer has the right to return your money with interest earned to that point. For example: A one-year callable CD means the *issuer* has the right to call the CD in and return your money with interest earned to that point. However the maturity date, at which time *you* have the right to remove your money may be much longer. It is not uncommon to see maturity dates of 10, 15, or even 20 years on callable CDs. If interest rates rise over the period, especially likely in today's low interest rate environment, you will be stuck with your lower-rate CD or pay a penalty to take your money out.
- **Are there call features and how do they work?** These can be quite tricky and confusing. Make sure you understand how the call features work. Call features benefit the issuer (bank), so beware of them if they recommend them to you. Understand that if interest rates go down, the issuer will most likely call the CD in and you will be stuck reinvesting those monies at the then–lower prevailing interest rates.
- **How much money will I get back if I redeem the CD before maturity?** This is another area for inquiry. You should not use these products if you need your money in the near future.

These products have significant charges if you redeem them early and may eat into your return, and even your principle

- **What are your reasons for recommending this product?** Don't let yourself fall victim to someone making a commission off you! They should have your interests at heart not their wallets on their mind.
- **How does this meet my financial objectives?** Every investment product should fit the overall goals of your investment profile.

Indexed-Linked CDs

One alternative to callable CDs is what is referred to as an Index-Linked CD. These CDs pay interest based on the performance of a stock index, like the S&P 500, usually with some minimum guaranteed interest rate over the life of the CD contract. They are structured so that you don't lose money[2] and if the market index performs well, you could earn far more than with a traditional fixed-rate CD. As long as you hold this CD to maturity you will not lose money, and you could earn a substantial market-related premium. However, if you need or want the money before the CD matures, you will lose money, and this penalty could erode your original principal.

Interest Penalties

Banks, credit unions, and savings and loans are in business to make money. If you buy a CD, the bank has to invest your money in ways that ensure that it earns enough to pay the interest rate they promised you, while also making money for themselves. This means that the bank may have to tie up its money to get a high enough rate of return to meet all of its obligations.

What does this mean for you? It means that the bank is going to charge you an early withdrawal penalty if you don't leave your money in the CD for as long as the originally agreed-upon term of the CD. This penalty varies, but it is generally three months interest

---

[2] Although, like any FDIC- or FSLIC-insured investment, only $250,000 in each eligible account at each bank or other institution is actually insured.

(for CDs that mature in less than one year) or six months interest (for CDs that mature in one year or more). It's also possible to lose some principal on these penalties if the penalty is greater than the amount of interest you've earned. For instance, if you cash in a five-year CD after six months, the penalty may exceed your earned interest and cut into your principal.

As long as you do proper planning to anticipate your income needs, these early withdrawal penalties will be avoided. Just make sure that the term of the CD you select matches up with your needs—don't take out a 5-year CD if you're going to need it in 6 months!

Interest Rate Risk

When you buy a (non-callable) CD, you are assuming (or gambling) that interest rates will remain stable or fall. This is especially true for longer duration (two year or longer) CDs. If you want to buy CDs but are concerned that interest rates will rise, you should do one of two things: Ladder the CDs (see the next section) or buy short-term CDs (12 months or less to maturity).

Short-term CDs allow you to earn some rate of interest while providing the liquidity you need for short-term expenses. Your money is not fully liquid, but it is not tied up for years, either.

Laddering CDs

A CD ladder is actually fairly simple. Instead of putting all of their available (income-generating) cash in long-term CDs, I have my clients buy a variety of CDs with staggered maturity dates. This means that every few months, some cash is being freed up (as a CD matures), and this cash, if not needed, can go into a longer-term CD, with the actual term determined by the trend in interest rates. If rates start rising there is always new money to put in these better-performing CDs, but if rates fall, there is still money earning a much higher interest rate.

Laddering CDs is an approach I recommend to increase my clients' investment flexibility and liquidity while maximizing current income in the short term. In a rising interest rate environment, such as the one we saw in 2004, this approach can maximize income and security of principal while maintaining the flexibility to respond to changing market and interest rate conditions.

Bethany came to me recently with concerns about her retirement income. She wanted to get a good return, with an eye toward eventually passing some money along to her kids. At the same time, she didn't want to subject her assets to unnecessary risks, and she also wanted to maintain a good level of liquidity. After going through her lifestyle expenses with her, I put the result in my roadmap worksheet to determine whether she had sufficient money in her operational accounts, in her emergency funds and long-term investments, and in her short-term fund (money she'll need within five years) before determining an investment plan for a long-term fund.

For her short-term fund, I decided to do some laddering. While she had originally planned to open a 5-year CD, I went through her lifestyle expenses and noted certain large purchases in her future—most notably, she planned to buy a new car—for which some liquidity would be prudent. I also noted that we were in the midst of an Inverted Yield Curve—a period in which long-term CDs were paying less interest than shorter-term CDs. As such, we opened up four CDs to start: a 6-month, a 12-month, an 18-month, and a 24-month. Typically we use increments of six months in laddering CDs so as to maximize return over the short term.

Every six months, another CD would come due. While we had the option of taking the money for any income needs she might have if she didn't need it, she could roll it into a new 24-month CD. After two years she would have four 24-month CDs, each set to come due every six months over the next two years! In so doing, we were able to improve her rate of return, while maintaining flexibility and liquidity for any unforeseen expenses that may arise. We can also do this with fixed income annuities (FIAs), though this is typically for a longer-term investment horizon.

CDs versus Fixed Annuities

Fixed annuities can be an attractive, tax-favored alternative to CDs for some retired (or soon-to-be-retired) investors. Which is best for you, though? The short answer is that it varies from person to person, and each has their benefits and drawbacks. Here is a rundown of some of the pros and cons of each, with some side-by-side comparisons of the two.

- Annuities allow your money to continue to grow tax-deferred.
- Annuities typically pay about 1 to 1.5 percent more for a similar guarantee period than CDs.
- Annuities are guaranteed by the insurance company that issues them—but this guarantee is only as strong as the insurance company itself.[3] (Always choose a company rated at least "A" by several rating companies.) CDs, by contrast, are insured by the FDIC or FSLIC.
- You can take withdrawals (usually up to 10 percent of the balance per year) from an annuity without penalties or charges. Cashing in a CD or an annuity before it matures results in considerable penalties, though some CDs give you the option of taking the interest as an income stream during the maturity. You must elect this option up front. Annuities allow for a guaranteed income stream to beneficiaries.
- If you die with an annuity still in deferral, the value goes directly to your named beneficiaries without passing through probate. The total amount that passes to your heirs is equal to your initial contributions, plus any interest earned, and minus any withdrawals you may have taken. Most CDs do have Payable-on-Death or Transfer-on-Death options, though these, too, must be elected up front.
- If you exercised an annuitization option, or you have an immediate annuity, it is the income stream that passes to your heirs. The payments are taxed on a favorable basis—pro rata based on your contributions and interest earned.
- You can annuitize the annuity contract and get a lifetime income. While the amount may not increase with inflation, it is a predictable and guaranteed income stream. However,

---

[3] Most states have what is known as a State Guarantee Fund, to which all insurance companies operating in the state contribute. The fund typically guarantees up to $100,000 of an annuity's value in the event that the company goes under. For more information on your state Guarantee Fund, contact your Insurance Commissioner's office.

there are annuities that have payouts that can be tied to a market index. In this scenario, the payments can increase.

- There are Indexed Annuities, and more recently developed Indexed CDs, that allow you to participate in stock market ups and virtually eliminate the market downs.

One Last Word About Indexed Annuities

Indexed Annuities have been maligned by some in the investment press who simply do not understand, or do not choose to understand, the way they work.

As illustrated in Exhibit 4.1, Three Worlds of Investing, the best solutions to attaining our financial goals will usually include all three worlds: the fixed world for safety and liquidity, the equity world for growth and future income, and the indexed world as an option for potentially higher returns than the world of safety, while still protecting your principal, and the option of future income.

In a recent article of the *Journal of Financial Planning*,[4] the authors take on much of the misinformation reported in the financial and investment press. They cite the errors by some journalists and industry professionals in these reports wherein it is posited that the market will always outperform Indexed Annuities. They further dispel the self-serving hypotheticals used in these reports and deal with real-world returns from real-world policies. This is simply done to dispel the notion that fixed index annuities cannot be competitive with other asset classes and to further show how the structure of fixed index annuities reduce their correlation to other asset classes.

As noted in the article, "The returns of real-world index annuities analyzed in this paper outperformed the S&P 500 Index over 67 percent of the time, and outperformed a 50/50 mix of one-year Treasury bills and the S&P 500 79 percent of the time."

The dangers in any such comparisons are data mining by selectively choosing time frames to support a particular position, and drawing any definitive conclusions based on the limited data

---

[4] Geoffrey VanderPal, D.B.A, CFP, CLU, CFS, RFC; Jack Marrion; and David Babbel, Ph.D. "Real-World Index Annuity Returns," *Journal of Financial Planning*. March 2011.

available. For example: To cite, as many in the investment industry do, that the average stock market return based on the S&P 500 over the last 84 years is 9.9 percent somehow supports investing in the market over other options, begs the question: Of what true value is that statistic? Show of hands: "How many of you intend to stay invested in the market for the next 84 years?"

The following explanation from *The Index Compendium* helps bring home that most critical ingredient to investment planning— *time*—especially when it comes to taking income from our portfolios. I deal with this in much greater detail in the next chapter, and how it relates to portfolio design. For now, notice how much chance plays into your investment planning for retirement. I have a fiduciary responsibility to my clients, which I take very seriously. Therefore, I look at whatever investment, insurance, and banking options, or combination thereof, will best serve my clients' needs and goals.

Exhibit 4.3 represents a graph for a 77-year-old with $100,000 who begins drawing $6,000 a year in distributions. The lines represent if they began taking returns in 2000, 2001, 2002 and so on. The numbers on the right show how much they would need in an average annual return to be able to withdraw $6,000 until they reach age 100. For instance, if this person began taking distributions in January 2000 they would require a 31.02 percent return on their money in order to have enough to be able to withdraw this amount for the remainder of their lifetime. If they retired in January 2001 they would need 17.96 percent, and so on. This chart shows the volatility of the market in relation to when you retire and begin taking distributions. As you can see, every year is different and this represents one of the potential pitfalls to the markets and why portfolio design and how it fits into your overall financial plan makes a dramatic difference for attaining your goals and maintaining your lifestyle.

Similarly, Exhibit 4.4 represents how timing affects how long your money lasts. This chart represents how long your money would last if you withdrew 6 percent annually, earned the S&P 500 annual returns and retired in 1960, 1961, and so on. This shows that there is a dramatic variation in the value of your portfolio that is completely dependent on chance. What a difference a year makes! Thus the importance of annuities comes into play because they can help eliminate this variation by providing fixed income streams.

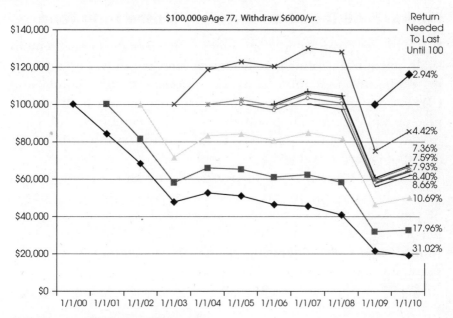

Exhibit 4.3   Retirement Roulette

Source: Index Compendium, February 2010, "Index Annuities Are the New Normal."

Exhibit 4.4   How Long Your Money Lasts Depends on Chance

If You Retired In	You Ran Out of Money In	Years Lasted
1960	1984	24
1961	1990	29
1962	1983	21
1963	1994	31
1964	1985	21
1965	1983	18
1966	1983	17
1967	1992	25
1968	1985	17
1969	1985	16
1970	1994	24
1971	2005	34
1972	1997	25
1973	1991	18

Data source: Index Compendium, February 2010, "Index Annuities Are the New Normal."

Putting It All Together: Investing for the Long Term

It takes careful planning to minimize your taxes during retirement while maximizing returns and maintaining liquidity. For many of my clients the best route is to use various annuities, bonds, and CDs to guarantee the safety of their principal and the level of their income while maintaining sufficient liquidity, combined with equities and equity-linked products, to attain sufficient growth to stay ahead of inflation and taxes.

The best plans provide for your liquidity and current income needs while allowing for growth to maintain the purchasing power of your long-term needs. One primary goal is always to seek the needed rate of return to maintain your desired lifestyle throughout your lifetime while minimizing risk. The next chapter shows you the safest way to invest in the market for the long term.

CHAPTER 5

How the Smart Money Invests

There are two times in a man's life when he should not speculate:
when he can't afford it and when he can.

—Mark Twain

Barry was 64 and rapidly approaching retirement when he came to me last year looking for financial guidance. As with all of my clients, I went through his current assets and worked with him to determine his projected lifestyle expenses. I found that if he invested prudently, using the academically researched and proven principles I recommend, he had enough money put away to assure a very comfortable retirement for himself and his wife. I explained to Barry that these principles would assure a measurable market return with minimal risk.

This was the first Barry had heard of these principles. His previous advisers had always proclaimed their ability to beat the market by picking the best mutual funds. They believed that the money managers at these mutual fund companies knew which stocks to buy and which to avoid, explaining that they had great track records that put them in the top percentile of money managers based on their past performance. In addition to their supposed stock-picking abilities, these same managers also boasted of their ability to time the market to get better returns and avoid losses.

Barry realized that his investment results were falling short of their big claims, and that the big ups and downs in his portfolio made it increasingly difficult to stay in the market. On top of this, he was being hurt by the fees and commissions associated with these funds, even as his advisers insisted that they had only a negligible impact on his financial situation. Each change of adviser just resulted in more of the same: an active management approach that ultimately resulted in more volatility and risk than he was willing to tolerate.

Finally, Barry came to me looking for a better way. I told him about my own experiences with investing, and how my principles could deliver the results he sought.

Learning through Trial and Error

The truth is, there was a time when I was caught up in a lot of the same misinformation that had misled Barry. I got my securities license almost 20 years ago and immediately went to the manager at my broker-dealer for guidance on which mutual fund managers to recommend.

"We've done a lot of analysis, and these are the proven performers," he said, handing me a list. "These are the guys who have consistently beaten the market over the last five or six years. If you want the best results for your clients, these are the mutual fund money managers you should be recommending."

I went ahead and began recommending these money managers to the clients who came to me seeking to invest in the market. To my surprise, these clients soon found themselves getting below-market returns despite investing with the mutual fund managers my broker-dealer had recommended. I was baffled: Were these proven performers just slumping, or had their luck simply run out? I also started to wonder if their favored status had more to do with their relationship with my broker-dealer than it did with their qualifications.

So I decided to start putting together my own portfolios of mutual funds. I once again looked at the top 10 percent of mutual funds in their respective asset categories based on performance over the last decade, but now I began implementing some of the principles of asset allocation that I'd learned in the course of my research. I blended large-, mid- and small-cap funds, and strived for a mix of domestic and international investments. The results were the same, even though I chased the top-performing funds. I found them eventually failing to deliver the consistent market returns that I sought. I started to realize that chasing past performance of mutual funds was a flawed way to develop an investing plan because most of these successful funds were simply promoting their luck rather than their expertise. Consequently this caused me to question the ability of actively managed funds to produce consistent above-market returns.

In the course of my research to find a better way to invest I came across the Eugene Fama and Kenneth French "Three Factor Model" for portfolio design. Fama and French didn't just make claims on the success of their strategies but showed the academic research behind their work. I diligently entered an intense three-year training program and absorbed as much information on investment strategies as possible. I learned the difference between active and passive management, and the perils of the former. I learned that it was folly to try and chase proven funds in an attempt to beat the market, and that I should instead aspire to simply attain market returns. I even learned that the fees and commissions that the fund managers had insisted were negligible were in fact taking a significant cut from the average investor's portfolio. Along the way, I rediscovered the real value of asset allocation, discipline, and how to achieve true diversification by applying these principles in portfolio design. I finally found the first investment philosophy that actually did what it said it could.

In other words, I learned that everything I thought I knew about active management was wrong.

The Real Story

It's true. For all the talk of stock picking and timing the market, there's really no secret to making big money on the stock market. If you're willing to put your money in the market and leave it there for an extended period of time (at least 10 years, and ideally 15), you can ride out the ups and downs and eventually see a real positive result—assuming, of course, that you've properly applied the principles I'll discuss shortly.[1] But in the short term, the stock market is far too volatile to consistently predict (see Exhibit 5.1). As David Booth, MBA, notes "A 3- or 5- or even 10-year period is too short a time to make very many statistical inferences from data."[2] Yes, you might get lucky and get some big returns. You might also lose a large percentage of your investments and find yourself forced to reduce your planned lifestyle.

Even if you apply all the principles I discuss in this chapter, there's still one secret ingredient to investing: *time*. And if you're close to the point where you'll need to take retirement income from your assets, time just isn't on your side. You can't afford to just stop taking income for 10 or 15 years, waiting for the stock market to recover from a bear market downturn. Yet, if you continue to take income, your portfolio may never recover its pre-bear market value. For this reason, I always advise my clients to minimize their exposure to market risk by segregating that part of their portfolio needed for income into fixed investments. They can then afford to leave that part of their portfolio designated for growth alone to ride out the ups and downs of the market.

Once you've stopped working, your priorities should shift from wealth accumulation to wealth preservation, with the ultimate goal of creating a reliable income stream from your portfolio that keeps pace with inflation, after taxes.

The question is: What is the best way to accomplish this?

Many investment advisers will start by giving you a risk tolerance test to determine how much risk (volatility) you can handle before you bail out of the market.

---

[1] The principle of buying a mutual fund or other investment vehicle and sticking with it through the market's ups and downs is commonly known as "buy-hold." Like the other principles of this investment strategy, though, it does not work in a vacuum. If you execute an investment strategy that doesn't properly utilize the principles of asset allocation and diversification, staying put won't magically give you a market result!

[2] David Booth, MBA, www.dfaus.com//library/bios/david_booth/index.html.

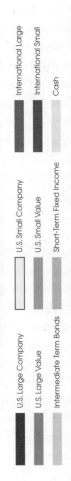

Exhibit 5.1 The Value of Diversification and Asset Classes with Low Correlation Based on the Best and Worst Performing Asset

Source: Matrix Asset Allocation.

However, risk tolerance is not the most important determining factor in putting together your portfolio—in fact, it should be the last thing you consider, as I'll illustrate.

One of the potential problems I have found with the risk tolerance approach is that investors tend to be a lot more optimistic sitting in the comfort of their adviser's office answering a questionnaire about hypothetical losses, than when they get a statement in the mail that shows a real-world loss of tens of thousands of dollars or more of their hard-earned money. This fact was really brought home by the recent bear market downturn from October of 2007 through March of 2009, and the increased volatility since then. Many investors, upon seeing the big losses in their portfolios, realized that maybe they weren't as risk tolerant as they originally thought! This becomes especially relevant for retirees who suddenly realize that their lifestyle and nest egg are now at risk. If they are dependent on income from their portfolio this is compounded even further, as they then require a higher return on their investments to maintain their lifestyle.

The other potential problem inherent in this approach is designing a portfolio that maximizes risk based on the perceived risk tolerance of the investor divined from the risk tolerance questionnaire. There is also the question of balancing the risk tolerance of couples. In my experience they rarely match up, and many times one spouse simply acquiesces to the spouse who has handled the investment responsibilities in the past.

Many times the investment adviser sees their primary goal for their clients as maximizing returns in proportion to the risk that their client can handle. For many retirees, this is simply the wrong approach. If you can have the lifestyle you want and cover your financial objectives without putting your assets at risk, why would you go all-out in an attempt to maximize returns and thereby jeopardize your retirement? Would you agree that a more suitable approach might be to design a portfolio around your needed rate of return while minimizing risk, primarily by choosing an appropriate ratio of equities and low-risk fixed investments?

During the 2004 presidential election, it was revealed that John Kerry and his wife Teresa had much of their half-billion-dollar fortune invested in municipal bonds, with very little in the market.

They already knew what I'm saying to you: If you don't need to take the risk, don't! (Of course with the potential problems facing municipal funds today, they might want to seek safer investments.)

The adviser should also ask you about your long-term investment goals. Think about how you would answer the following questions:

- How long do you intend to invest?
- What percentage of your total assets are you investing?
- Will you need income from your portfolio and if so when?
- Do you have other funds set aside for emergencies?
- What, if any, tax consequences need to be considered? (Remember, it is not only about how much you make but how much you get to keep!)

All of these steps are part of the process of determining the suitability of the asset allocation strategy and the actual assets that will be used.

As detailed in Chapters 1 and 2, my process starts with these questions and more in developing a comprehensive financial game plan: We determine what your financial needs and goals are and what rate of return you'll require from your investments to meet those goals. Next, I work with you to develop an investment strategy that will attain that needed rate of return, seeking to thus minimize risk and volatility. As I mentioned before, we consider the risk tolerance issue last. At this point, the vast majority of my clients are relieved to find themselves well within their risk tolerance.

To help you implement that strategy requires properly utilizing the principles of asset allocation, diversification, and discipline. While there is no way to eliminate risk entirely and no way to beat the market consistently (as research proves), a prudent asset allocation strategy can go a long way toward minimizing the risk to your principal and getting the market returns you seek.

Starting Off: The Retirement Investor Quiz

When it comes to the stock market there's a lot of misinformation out there that can trip you up. Before you even think about buying a stock, it's time to test your own knowledge and dispense with some of the common myths.

The Retirement Investor Quiz

1. Are any of your assets invested in the stock market, either directly in a non-qualified or IRA account, or in a retirement account through your employer?
2. Do you know what the needed rate of return is to meet your retirement needs?
3. What is the net (after costs) annualized rate of return on your portfolio?
4. What is the potential risk/volatility in your portfolio?
5. How much does your portfolio earn relative to the market?
6. How diversified is your portfolio?
7. Do you know what the Markowitz Efficiency Frontier is?
8. Do you know where your portfolio falls on the Markowitz Efficiency Frontier (gives you the lowest risk for a given level of return)?
9. When you make decisions related to your investment portfolio, do you know what you are doing and why you are doing it?
10. Are you currently using or considering consulting with a financial professional you trust with your financial future?

Now for one final question: How confident were you in answering these questions? Did some of them give you pause, or make you stop and think about how much you really know about your investments? However you answered them, the information I have compiled in this chapter may even help those of you who answered confidently and consider yourself to be savvy, knowledgeable investors. If you plan to be in the market, I want you to know how the smart money invests.

Busting the Investment Myths

Let's start off by addressing some of the investment myths that are making it difficult for many people to intelligently invest.

Myth 1: Stocks Can Be Picked in Such a Way As to Beat The Market

Most stockbrokers will tell you that there's a way to beat the market—and that they have the secret to doing so, of course. Yet, if you look at the most recent research, you'll find that only about 10 percent or less of active U.S. equity mutual fund managers beat the average return of the S&P 500. For people who make a living picking stocks, those aren't very good results! The reason is pretty simple: Since stock prices basically reflect all available information, it's more or less impossible to consistently beat the market. Famed economist Eugene Fama once said that, "In an efficient market, at any point in time the actual price of a security will be a good estimate of its intrinsic value."[3]

It's also worth noting that the statistics put out by the mutual fund companies don't tell the whole story, as they reflect what is known as survivorship bias. This refers to the tendency of companies to kill the worst-performing mutual funds over the course of the year and remove their results when calculating overall performance. According to the Center for Research in Security Prices, over 32,000 mutual funds have been born since 1923, but just over 20,000 remain. The big losses posted by these nearly 12,000 dead funds are swept under the rug. To illustrate the point—the 200 worst dead funds posted an average loss of 73.9 percent.[4]

When we factor these dead funds back into the equation, the perils of stock picking become clearer. The average U.S. equity mutual fund from 1973 to 2009 would have grown a $100,000 portfolio to a little under $2 million. However, if that $100,000 had simply been invested in the S&P 500 Index, we would be looking at over $3.1 million—a difference of nearly $1.2 million—over 50 percent more! Clearly, trying to pick stocks does more harm than good. See Exhibit 5.2.

Myth 2: The Track Record of a Fund or Fund Manager Is the Best Way to Predict How the Investment Will Do in the Future

Usually the best-performing funds one year are often nowhere to be found the next year. As Exhibit 5.3 shows, the top 30 funds from

[3]"Random Walks in Stock Market Prices," *Financial Analysts Journal* 51, no. 1 (September–October 1965), http://citeseerx.ist.psu.edu/viewdoc/download?doi=10.1.1.74.7408&rep=rep1&type=pdf.
[4]Center for Research in Security Prices, Survivor-Bias-Free U.S. Mutual Fund Guide, www.crsp.com/documentation/pdfs/mfdb_guide.pdf.

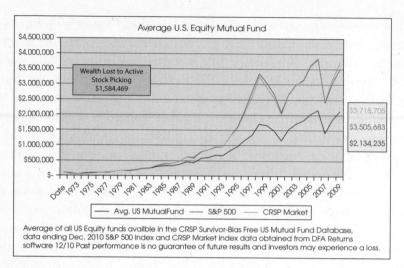

Average U.S. Equity Mutual Fund

Wealth Lost to Active Stock Picking $1,584,469

$3,718,705
$3,505,683
$2,134,235

Avg. US MutualFund — S&P 500 — CRSP Market

Average of all US Equity funds availble in the CRSP Survivor-Bias Free US Mutual Fund Database, data ending Dec. 2010 S&P 500 Index and CRSP Market Index data obtained from DFA Returns software 12/10 Past performance is no guarantee of future results and investors may experience a loss.

Exhibit 5.2   Wealth Lost to Active Stock Picking

Exhibit 5.3   Track Record Investing

	1988–1997	1998–2007
Top 30 Funds Average Return	23.13	6.20
All Funds Average Return	15.82	6.98
S&P 500 Index	18.86	7.23

Source: Micropal Group Limited.

1988 to 1997 actually got below-average (and below-market) returns in the next 10-year period. This goes to show that the success of a given fund manager is indicative of little more than luck—luck that will eventually run out. Indeed, in looking at the success of U.S. large-blend mutual funds (which invest in large well-established companies) and their ability to beat the S&P 500 Index, Morningstar Principia Software found that active managers' performance was worse than what would be expected by chance.

Myth 3: Some People and Advisers Can Successfully Time the Market—They Know When to Get in and When to Get out

There is overwhelming statistical evidence that this approach has never worked as a long-term strategy and is rarely successful in the short term. Charles D. Ellis, managing partner of Greenwich

Associates and professor at both the Harvard Business School and Yale School of Management, wrote in his book *Investment Policy*: "The evidence on investment managers' success with market timing is impressive—and overwhelmingly negative."[5] A study by Dalbar Inc. found that between 1988 and 2007, market-timer investors saw an average loss of 1.35 percent.

Also beware of the common euphemisms for market timing. A mutual fund manager might tell you that he or she practices strategic allocation or that they are heavy in cash right now. What they're really saying is that they are chasing what they believe to be trends in certain asset classes—for instance, investing heavily in bonds because they seem to be on the rise at the moment. As I'll show in the section on asset allocation, your goal should be to blend different asset classes to minimize risk—not to pick one or the other in pursuit of perceived short-term trends.

Myth 4: The Costs Associated with An Investment Do Not Matter As Long As the Returns Are Good

Actually, the long-term effect of these costs can seriously erode your investment performance. The most visible of these costs are commissions and 12b-1 fees (a marketing cost). If you are investing through a variable annuity, there are additional costs to consider (see Chapter 4). In a bull market, people are less likely to notice or care about the impact of these costs—what's a few percentage points if you're getting double digit returns, right? In a bear market, though, people stand up and take notice that they're losing money on top of the market losses they're already incurring. The fact is, the impact of these costs should always be your concern!

Commissions and fees are only the surface of what you are really charged. There are also hidden costs, such as trading costs related to portfolio turnover. The higher the portfolio turnover, the higher these transaction costs get. One example is known as the bid/ask spread. When there is a difference between what the

---

[5]Charles Ellis, *Investment Policy* (Burr Ridge, IL; Irwin Professional Publishing, 1985).

seller asks and what the buyer bids, the difference goes to the market makers—when you see a picture of the floor of the stock exchange, all those people running around in the colored jackets are the market maker reps. These people make the spread and benefit when your mutual fund manager places a buy or sell order at a given price. While this cost never shows up on the reports you receive from your fund manager you can rest assured that it's there and eating into your returns.

While it may amount to less than a dollar per share, these hidden costs can really pile up. Dr. Charles Ellis found that investors could easily be paying the equivalent of 3 to 7 percent of their assets a year without ever realizing the extent of the costs involved.[6] Look at it this way: To make up for these hidden costs, these active fund managers would have to beat the market by this 3 to 7 percent margin just to make all their trading worth it. And as we've seen, that's not something they can do on a consistent basis. As Dr. Ellis himself put it: "How much better must a[n] . . . [actively trading] . . . manager be to at least recover the cost of . . . [portfolio turnover]? The answer is daunting."[7]

Active Management

The myths listed above all pertain to the practice of active management—going out and actively picking stocks rather than, say, investing in an index. Benjamin Graham, a mentor to Warren Buffett, co-wrote the book on stock picking, *Security Analysis*,[8] in 1934, but he eventually recognized that technological advances had virtually eliminated the kind of informational asymmetry that made stock picking possible. "I am no longer an advocate of elaborate techniques of security analysis in order to find superior value opportunities," he said in a 1976 interview. "[Today] I doubt whether such

---

[6]Ibid.

[7]Ibid.

[8]Graham, Benjamin. *The Intelligent Investor: The Classic Bestseller on Value Investing with an Introduction and Appendix by Warren E. Buffett.* New York: Harper Collins Publishers, Inc, 1973.

extensive efforts will generate sufficiently superior selections to justify their cost."[9]

Ben Graham's most famous student, Warren Buffett, has likewise preached the folly of active management practices. In his 1993 letter to Berkshire Hathaway shareholders, Buffett wrote; "By periodically investing in an index fund, the know-nothing investor can actually outperform most investment professionals." The following story is an excerpt from a speech Buffett gave at Columbia University in 1984 that appeared in the index of Ben Graham's book, *The Intelligent Investor*, Fourth Edition. In it he imagined a nationwide contest in which 225 million Americans would wager a dollar on the flip of a coin; those getting heads would win a dollar from those guessing wrong and would stay in the contest and those getting tails were out. After 20 flips, you'd have about 215 very lucky people who had successfully called their coin flips. By this exercise each would have turned one dollar into a little over $1 million.

Now, wrote Buffett, imagine that some of these 215 people would probably write books on "How I Turned a Dollar into a Million in Twenty Days Working 30 Seconds a Morning." They would tackle skeptical professors with "If it can't be done why are there 215 of us?"

To take the story a step further: What if they went into business, touting their incredible skill at coin-flipping and promising to show others how they could increase their wealth by doing the same for them?

It sounds ridiculous, but it would be a lot like what we have now: An entire industry of self-proclaimed experts beat the market over some specified period of time *not* by skill but rather by sheer chance. Whatever their track record, successful active fund managers are no more skilled at picking stocks than these hypothetical coin-flippers are at predicting coin flips.[10]

---

[9]A Conversation with Benjamin Graham. www.bylo.org/ngraham76.html
[10]Buffett, Warren E. "The Superinvestors of Graham-and-Doddsville." www.valueinvesting.de/en/superinvestors.htm

Tune Out the Media's Advice

Mutual fund managers aren't the only people who make a living from active management, as outlined in the myths listed above. There are countless experts in the media who write books and host TV shows, loudly proclaiming the wisdom of their approach and directing their audience to buy or sell given stocks. The important thing to remember is that whatever their credentials or profile, these people are not in the business of making you money—they're in the business of making themselves money. After all, a TV personality who preaches patience and passive management practices won't last long in the business. People want to hear how to get rich quick!

Investing versus Speculating: Know the Difference!

While many of these active mutual fund managers will refer to what they do as investing, these stock picking practices are better characterized as speculating. Ben Graham summarized the difference as such: "An investment operation is one which, upon thorough analysis, promises safety of principal and an adequate return. Operations not meeting these requirements are speculative."

Speculating can be defined as purchasing investment vehicles (such as stocks, bonds, and real estate) with the sole intention of profiting from fluctuations in price. Sometimes referred to as a legitimate, socially acceptable form of gambling, speculation may prove profitable for some but disastrous for others. Much like going to the racetrack, casino, or betting large sums on sports, it can become a very risky habit.

Many people purchase stocks or mutual funds based on the advice of their stockbroker or another investment adviser. They may also consult television programs, magazines, and newspapers, or perhaps receive a hot tip from a friend, colleague, family member, or neighbor. This approach is based on seeking out stocks or mutual funds that will give some phenomenal return on investment. However, these investments are purchased from various sources at different times, chasing unrealistic returns with little or no thought given to portfolio design or the principles of investing

I have mentioned. The result is high volatility, premium trading costs, diminished returns, and, quite possibly, heavy losses.

There is another way, though. As I have said before, investing in the stock market for an extended period of time and applying the intelligent approach that I'll discuss shortly will always give the investor the market return they want. While speculating is risky and unreliable, investing is the precise, prudent, life-long quest to progressively build wealth. In the next section, I show you how to do it.

A Real Story About Speculative Investing

Ask yourself a question: When you are retired, or near retired, can you afford to lose 40 to 50 percent of your retirement nest egg? If you are, or will be, dependent on this money, how will a loss like this affect your income stream and subsequently your financial future? The answer could be devastating. This is not just conjecture, since many investors experienced declines of this magnitude in 2008.

I once worked with a couple who were forced to come to terms with this very reality. The couple, who handled their own investments, moved to Tennessee from another state and retained the investment broker they had been using for years. The husband liked researching his investments, spending hours a week trying to find the best investments in the market. During the bull market of the 1990s, he did fairly well, reaping a large enough return to grow their nest egg and supplement their income. Life was good until 2000, when the husband fell ill and was diagnosed with cancer. He was no longer able to spend the time on his investments as before, so the wife relied on their broker to make all the decisions.

The husband passed away and the wife continued to work with the broker, since that was how it had always been. She still drew income from their investments despite the fact that the value of their portfolio was decreasing. By the time she called me to discuss her estate plan, their portfolio had already shrunk to half its size. I was put in the unenviable position of telling her what her broker had not. My news to her was that, if she continued on her current path, she would run out of money in about five to seven years. This wasn't something a widowed woman in her early 60s wanted to hear.

With what little income she had, she needed to either drastically downsize her home to free up cash to invest for income, or re-enter the workforce. Unfortunately she did not listen to my advice, instead choosing to stick with her stockbroker. She eventually lost most of her nest egg and wound up having to move in with her daughter.

My heart went out to her because she had been put in such a difficult position. Had they invested in the way that I'm recommending in this chapter, she would not have ended up in such a predicament.

Is It Ever Okay to Speculate?

My father-in-law liked to gamble, and he would occasionally go down to the racetrack to put money on horses or to the casino to play the slot machines. He recognized, however, that risking any significant amount of his assets on a horse race or one-armed bandit was a recipe for disaster. As such, he always set aside a small amount of money for his trips to the race track or the casino—the same as one would set aside money for a vacation or other form of entertainment—it was in his budget and he would never risk his nest egg in such a manner.

It's fine to take the same attitude with speculating. Some people simply enjoy playing the stock market and seeing if they can chase big returns. As long as this is not the foundation of your investment strategy, and you don't subject a significant amount of your nest egg to the inherent risks of active management, it's okay to speculate a little on the side. Indeed, I encourage those clients who expressed a desire to try their hand at speculating in the stock market to set up a small online brokerage account—for them it is like any other hobby one may set aside money for.

As for my father-in-law, he never got into speculating in the stock market. He thought it was too risky!

The Smart Money Investment Strategy

Now that I've discussed what not to do, let's talk about how the smart money invests. In my office, this starts with the Confidential Lifestyle Questionnaire and Lifestyle Expense Worksheet I have every client complete. In addition, I complete the Comprehensive

Lifestyle Fact Finder with them to gather all the necessary information about their specific financial life. (See the Appendices in this book.)

When it comes to putting together a portfolio, my decisions are based on your income (both present and projected), assets, expenses, tax concerns, inflation, and overall financial goals. This helps me determine the needed rate of return on your investment portfolio. I then use a Monte Carlo simulation from a software program that uses numerous variables—including the rate of inflation, the market rate of return, and tax rates—to compute and provide an estimate of the statistical likelihood of successfully attaining your financial goals. From this, I put together a plan that focuses on minimizing—and as much as possible eliminating—risk so that you can attain the needed return for your retirement plans.

The Monte Carlo Simulation

The Monte Carlo Simulation allows you to see how the effects of market volatility could affect your retirement plan. While it cannot predict your financial future, the Monte Carlo Simulation accounts for how fluctuations in inflation, tax rates, and rates of return may affect your portfolio. It does so by assigning your portfolio a standard deviation; in other words, it attributes a value that determines the riskiness of your portfolio based on the allocation of your assets. Ultimately, the simulation provides you with multiple scenarios so you can judge how well your portfolio will react to different economic situations.

Here's how it works:

- The simulation uses different inflation, tax rates, and rates of return for each year of your hypothetical financial plan.
- 10,000 full financial plan calculations are conducted to determine 10,000 possible future financial market environments.
- These results—including highs, lows, and averages—offer indications about a potential plan's performance because the calculations take a number of broad market conditions into account.
- Included are capital assets (tax-advantaged and taxable), expenses, pension benefits, and Social Security benefits.
- This simulation offers insights into the shape, trends, and potential range of future retirement plan outcomes within volatile market conditions.

In putting together this plan, I rely on the three fundamental principles of investing and the Smart Money Investment Strategy:

1. Asset allocation
2. Diversification
3. Discipline

All About Asset Allocation

In "The Determinants of Portfolio Performance," the investment experts Gary Brinson, Randolph Hood, and Gilbert Beebower made a startling discovery: they found that stock selection accounts for only 4 percent of portfolio performance. Market timing—when you get in and out of the market—is even less important, accounting for only 2 percent of performance. The other 94 percent of portfolio performance is determined by asset allocation.[11]

So what is asset allocation, and why is it so important?

Quite simply, asset allocation is about blending certain asset classes of stocks and bonds with a negative correlation (when one rises the other falls and vice versa) in such a way as to get your desired market return while minimizing risk. This is illustrated in the Markowitz Efficient Frontier, which shows the areas of lowest risk and highest return. (See Exhibit 5.4.)

In addition, if asset allocation is done correctly within the portfolio design—building on the foundation set by Modern Portfolio Theory as illustrated in Markowitz's Efficient Frontier (which maximizes expected returns for any level of volatility), and incorporating the Three-Factor Model utilized in Free Market Portfolio Theory—it can greatly reduce your volatility while still attaining the market rate of return you're seeking.

Many financial advisers and stockbrokers talk about the benefits of asset allocation and diversification in the structure of your investment portfolio. The question is: Do they properly apply these principles? Asset allocation is not just about blending stocks/equities, bonds/fixed, and money markets/cash in a portfolio. The next very

---

[11]Gary P. Brinson, L. Randolph Hood, and Gilbert L. Beebower, "Determinants of Portfolio Performance," *Financial Analysts Journal* (January/February 1995): 51.

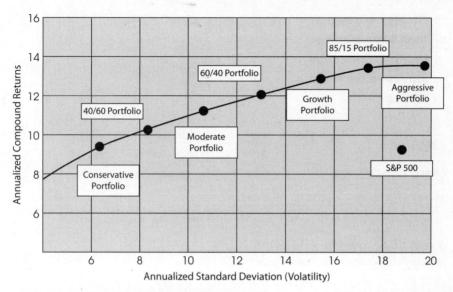

Exhibit 5.4   Markowitz Efficient Frontier
Source: Edinformatics, The Capital Asset Pricing Model—Fundamental Analysis,
www.edinformatics.com/investor_education/capital_asset_pricing_model.htm.

important step in asset allocation is to determine the asset classes represented in the stock/equity part of your portfolio and in what proportions.

Asset Allocation and the Three-Factor Model

Dr. Eugene Fama and Dr. Kenneth French took Modern Portfolio Theory to its logical conclusion by showing that certain asset classes tend to negatively correlate, and should therefore be chosen in tandem as part of an asset allocation strategy. These three factors are:

1. The Market Factor—stocks versus bonds (see Exhibit 5.5)
2. The Size Factor—small cap versus large cap stocks
3. The Value Factor—growth stocks versus value stocks

This three-factor model built on the work of Harry Markowitz, William Sharpe, and Merton Miller to create Free Market Portfolio Theory.

- **Equities are riskier than fixed income.**
- **Equities historically provide a higher rate of return.**

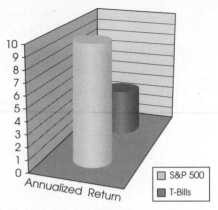

1926–2009	S&P 500$_{1,7}$	T-Bills
Annualized Return	9.81	3.66
Standard Deviation	20.51	3.08

Note: Past performance is no guarantee of future results and investors may experience a loss.

Exhibit 5.5   The Market Factor
Source: DFA Returns Software, December 2009.

Fama and French now sit on the board of directors of Dimensional Fund Advisers, an investment firm that creates institutional funds based on Modern Portfolio Theory. Today, DFA works with Matson Money in Cincinnati to create portfolios that can only be accessed by advisers such as me. Far from being limited to the annals of economic research, the work of Fama and French is still used to create the portfolios I recommend for my clients and that I invest in personally!

How Do You Measure Diversification?

When I have a new client with money in the stock market, one of the first things I do is to perform a free market portfolio analysis, which allows me to show how their portfolio stacks up to the free market portfolios I recommend. To measure diversification, I look at how many unique holdings they have—that is, how many unique stocks are in the portfolio, and how many times they hold the same stocks in multiple mutual funds—*not* just how many total stocks they hold. Often I find that there is significant overlap, to the point that of the 3,000 total stocks in their mutual funds, only about 1,000 are unique—in actively managed funds this can be a moving target as active managers are always buying and selling stocks. In the portfolios that I recommend, there is no overlap between funds. These portfolios will have over 12,000 unique stock holdings—that is because the portfolios that I recommend use no-load institutional funds designed to capture proven asset classes that provide the greatest return with the least amount of risk.

The Importance of Staying Disciplined

Have you ever heard about the importance of staying invested from your adviser? When your portfolio is down at given times, especially during bear markets, as in 2000 through 2002 and most recently in 2008, did your adviser stress the importance of holding course with your investment plan?

Yet, at the same time, do they call you regularly to recommend that you buy or sell certain of your holdings? Is this same adviser, who may stress the importance of staying disciplined, recommending changing your portfolio year in and year out?

Do you also see the managers of your mutual funds or managed accounts regularly buying and selling stocks and bonds within those funds and/or accounts?

Do you know what the turnover ratios of your individual holdings are?

As noted earlier in this chapter, this adds cost to your portfolio, which reduces your net return. Beyond that, how do they justify preaching discipline, when they obviously don't practice it?

When I was a child my parents had a saying: "Do as I say, not as I do." That may have been appropriate at times when, as a young child I was trying to emulate risky adult behavior, though how much better it would have been for them to lead by example. As a responsible, reasonably intelligent, somewhat successful adult, I have to question the motives of such contradictions in the advice of those making investment decisions and recommendations in my behalf. Is it truly for my benefit, or theirs?

The bottom line is, if you have a properly constructed portfolio and investment plan based on your current financial needs and goals using the principles outlined here, there is no reason or need to change your portfolio, unless your underlying financial needs or goals change; in fact changing your portfolio would be counterproductive.

Discipline is about holding course when you know you have the right plan, and your advisers and money managers should be following that same advice. Actively buying and selling stocks and bonds in your portfolio year in and year out not only adds costs, and thereby reduces your net investment returns, it also increases risk of loss and negative volatility.

Part of my job is to help my clients stay disciplined, to protect their plan. One of my favorite prayers is known as the Serenity Prayer:

"God grant me the Serenity to accept the things I cannot change, the Courage to change the things I can, and the Wisdom to know the difference."

Discipline is about having the serenity to accept the inevitable ups and downs of the market, the courage to make changes only when required by life changes (as in nearing retirement or entering the distribution phase of our lives), and thereby the wisdom to know when to hold course and when to act.

Tax Planning and Investments

While tax considerations for IRAs are covered extensively in Chapter 3, here are some further points to keep in mind when considering the tax impact on your investments:

- Money that you accumulated for retirement in tax-deferred retirement accounts is normally taxed at ordinary income tax rates. These rates may be significantly higher than long-term capital gains rates.
- Some retirement investments are not taxed. These sources include money in a Roth IRA and the after-tax contributions, if any, you made to a traditional IRA.
- The funds in annuities are taxed at ordinary income tax rates. The exception is any money you put in that was already taxed.
- Money you have accumulated in non-retirement stock, bond, CD, and mutual fund portfolios is taxed in different ways:
    - Long-term capital gains in stocks and stock mutual funds are taxed at (more) favorable capital gains rates.

◆ Interest income from taxable bonds, CDs, money market accounts, and other bank accounts is normally taxed as ordinary income.

◆ Income from tax-free bonds is not taxed by the federal government but may be taxed by your state, city, or other entity.

◆ Dividends from bonds may qualify for favorable lower tax rates.

Most importantly, tax laws and tax rates are constantly changing. That's why it is so important to consult a tax professional on the tax projections you and any advisers make before making an investment decision.

Here is an example that often helps my clients understand how tax planning can play an important role in their investment strategy. Let's say you have $100,000 in a traditional (tax-deferred) IRA, and another $100,000 in a non-qualified account. Applying the principles I've laid out in this chapter, in this example, we elect for a balanced portfolio with 50 percent in U.S. stocks and 50 percent in bonds.

I have had many prospective clients come into my office with balanced portfolios in which the tax qualified accounts (IRAs) and the non-qualified accounts are treated the same when their objective is a balanced portfolio, 50 percent stocks and 50 percent bonds. However, there is a better way. Knowing your IRA money is going to be taxed at ordinary income tax rates no matter what you invest in, why not invest it in bonds, as the interest income from bonds is also taxed at higher ordinary income tax rates? Then use the non-qualified money to invest in stocks, which will then be eligible for lower long-term capital gains tax rates when you sell them. (Keep in mind you will need to hold the stocks for over a year to qualify for long-term capital gains rates. If you sell them after holding them for less than a year, they would be considered short-term capital gains and taxed at ordinary income tax rates.) In my example this would have the $100,000 in the IRA be invested in bonds and the $100,000 in the non-qualified account invested in stocks, still accomplishing the overall objective of a balanced portfolio with 50 percent in stocks and 50 percent in bonds. See Exhibit 5.6.

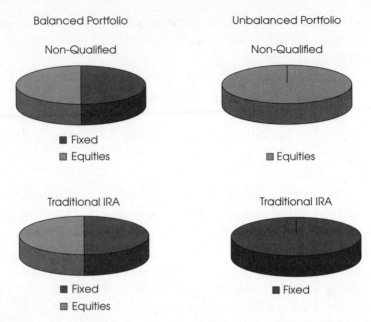

Exhibit 5.6   Comparing Investment Strategies: Unbalanced Portfolio versus Balanced Portfolio

Here's another example that would be an exception: You still have $100,000 in a non-qualified account, but this time the other $100,000 is in a Roth IRA. Should you put your Roth money in fixed investments or equities?

On the one hand, the same tax advantage from the previous example still applies: Putting your non-qualified money in equities means that it will potentially be taxed at the lower long-term capital gains rate. However, this time, you have the opportunity for tax-free growth through the Roth IRA, and though tax deferred growth and lower capital gains rates are good, tax-free is even better. Keep in mind that equities historically have outperformed fixed over the long haul.

To put it another way, if you have the opportunity for tax-free growth, you should make the most of it, and making the most of it in this example would be to maximize the tax-free growth of the Roth IRA by investing it in stocks. Especially when you consider it is best to preserve tax-free Roth distributions as the last money you will ever use. One last caveat, which holds true here as throughout the book: For every rule there is an exception to the rule, and an exception to the exception! Your situation is unique and requires in-depth analysis as to which of these strategies or combination of strategies will work best for you.

My Best Advice

Remember, there is no such thing as a one-size-fits-all ideal portfolio. Every investor is unique and the allocation of their investments should reflect that. I work closely with my clients to ensure that they are truly comfortable with their investment choices.

There is also no surefire way to guarantee everything about an investment, [the closest possibly being Treasury Inflation-Protected Securities (TIPS)] but there are ways to reduce your risk. If you do nothing else, please consider the following investment advice:

- Follow an asset allocation approach that fits your needs and risk tolerance level. Make sure your portfolio is rebalanced on a regular quarterly basis to maintain your asset allocation, and for tax management (effectively capturing and balancing capital gains and losses).
- Practice real diversification—don't just buy a variety of mutual funds and think you're diversified, make sure you are diversified by asset class.
- Greatly reduce your investments in stocks, stock mutual funds, stock ETFs, and so on, as you approach the age at which you'll need retirement income. Time is no longer on your side!
- As always, work with a financial professional who shares your investment philosophy.

Looking Forward

Now that we have a solid financial foundation it is time to look at an area of potential risk that could sabotage all that you have worked so hard to create, and rob you of your financial freedom.

In the next chapter we take a realistic look at the risk of long-term care. I will help you determine the probability and the potential net cost of the various options for providing the differing levels of care. Most important, we will explore strategies to minimize the impact on your finances and provide peace of mind for your family.

CHAPTER 6

Paying for Helping Hands

THE INS AND OUTS OF LONG-TERM CARE

If I knew I was going to live this long, I would have taken better care of myself.

—Mickey Mantle

There was a time when families frequently provided the care necessary for their aging parents and grandparents, but times are changing. When I was 14 years old, my maternal grandmother moved in with us. My mom—all of five feet and 90 pounds—took care of Grandma as best she could for as long as possible, converting our living room into a bedroom because Grandma was not able to climb the stairs. Unfortunately, Grandma had Parkinson's Disease, and at the time treatment options were very limited. On top of this, my mother was raising six children between the ages of 4 and 14, which made it even more difficult to find time to provide the high level of care my grandmother needed. After a couple of years, my grandmother's deteriorating condition made it physically impossible for my mother to provide the level of care Grandma needed. My parents instead found a nursing home that could meet my grandmother's needs.

As you near retirement, it's important to consider how your health care needs will evolve as you grow older, what your long-term care options will be, and how you will pay if long-term care becomes necessary. The costs of long-term health care can be devastating and any financial planning strategy that does not account for the possibility of long-term health care costs is a recipe for disaster.

What Are Your Options?

Long-term health care need not be limited to nursing homes. Depending on your health and financial situation, there may be numerous options available to you.

Staying Home

Most people would like to stay at home as long as possible. Today, there are numerous Home Health Care options available for those who have planned accordingly.

My wife's parents had more than their share of health issues. My father-in-law's diabetes caused him numerous problems—from failing eyesight to kidney problems that forced him to be on dialysis for years before he finally received a kidney transplant. My mother-in-law developed a form of polyneuropathy that caused her to lose feeling in her arms and legs and took away her ability to do simple, everyday tasks. The neuropathy also affected her lungs to the point that she had to be on oxygen on a 24/7 basis.

While my father-in-law received Medicare and had a supplemental health plan as part of his retirement benefits, there was no coverage for nonskilled Home Health Care. Fortunately, they planned well and were able to pay the costs from their savings.

The Trend of Assisted Living

As two people who devoted their lives to caring for others—my father-in-law was a cardiologist and my mother-in-law was a stay-at-home mom who raised two children—it was particularly difficult for them to increasingly lose their independence. Though my wife and her sister helped as much as possible, they both lived in different states and had jobs and children. Like other folks I work with, my in-laws did not want to be a burden to their families. They wanted to take care of themselves and, God willing, stay at home as long as they wished. The rest of my family and I committed ourselves to doing everything possible to make their wishes come true.

When staying at home is no longer an option, though, assisted living is an increasingly attractive option for those who are no longer able to live on their own. I have a client in her late 80s, Sarah, whose eyesight had been failing for years. It eventually got to the point that she became a danger to herself—she began to leave the stove on unknowingly, and her daughter Linda was worried that she might trip over something and injure herself seriously. A few years ago, she and her daughter decided it was time to find an assisted living facility, and called me for any help I could provide in finding a suitable home in the area.

After visiting a few locations, I chose a facility that best fit their needs and arranged to take a tour with Sarah and Linda. We had lunch there, met with the Activity Director, and looked at the available apartments. They were able to choose an apartment they really liked and I helped to negotiate a price that further reduced their costs. Linda had some of her mom's furniture and personal belongings moved in and arranged to make the apartment feel as much like home as possible. Sarah was thrilled with the food, the people, and the activities, and after a few months told me she would have moved sooner had she known how nice it was going to be. Fortunately, through good planning, she was able to cover the costs without any worry.

Planning Ahead

While you and your spouse may never need long-term care, it's always best to plan for the worst and hope for the best. You need to carefully assess the likelihood of needing long-term care, and plan your finances accordingly. One of the main goals of financial retirement planning is to develop an assured income stream. If you fail to factor in the potential for needing long-term care, the cost can wind up far exceeding the income stream you have established.

In assessing the potential for long-term care, there are a number of factors to consider. First, people are living longer than ever before, and approximately one in three people over the age of 65 will require some form of long-term care. If you are married, there is a good chance that at least one of you will need long-term care at some point.

Second, it's important to think about what kind of long-term care you and your spouse would like to receive. Most people would like to get help at home or in a continuing care/assisted living community. Long-term care may also be provided in a group setting (especially for dementia patients) or as adult day care. Adult day care is particularly valuable if you hope to continue to live semi-independently (for instance, with the assistance of a son or daughter who works full time).

Finally, consider your personal health situation and family health history to help determine the likelihood of needing long-term care. If many of your close family members have needed long-term care (LTC), your chances are probably much greater than someone whose relatives have lived to ripe old ages and still been active, healthy, and independent. Still, medical and family histories can only go so far, and it's unwise to assume that you'll remain healthy as you grow older.

One of the primary focuses of my practice and the main reason I am writing this book is to show people how to structure their assets and income to meet their needs and goals in retirement. There are ways to set up your assets so as to protect you and your spouse's lifestyles as you pay for long-term care. However, it takes a new way of looking at financial planning and money management, as well as careful analysis of your personal financial situation.

Common Myths About Long-Term Care

It's common for new clients to not to have done any research about long-term care—after all no one wants to think about not being able to take care of themselves or their spouses. As such, many of these clients come in with some common misconceptions about long-term care.

Myth 1: You Will Never Need LTC Long-Term Care

Many people simply refuse to face the fact they may need LTC in the future without first evaluating their personal situation—their family support, personal and family medical history, and financial state. While some people choose to put on blinders and tell themselves that they won't need LTC, the fact is that LTC is not all that rare. According to the U.S. Department of Health and Human Services, this year about 9 million people over the age of 65 will need long-term care services and by 2020 that number will increase to 20 million.[1]

None of us can know ahead of time which of these categories we are going to fall into. It is a lot easier to make plans now for the possibility of LTC; if you wind up needing it, you'll be glad you planned ahead.

Myth 2: Medicare Will Pay Your Bills

Many retirees may assume that Medicare will pay for their LTC needs. In fact, Medicare benefits for long-term care are very limited and based on very strict guidelines. The most you'll ever get is 100 days per incident and, according to a study conducted by the U.S. Administration for Aging Medicare, Medicare only paid about 9 percent of total LTC costs in 1995. Assuming Medicare is going to pay for all care needs is one of the biggest retirement planning mistakes I see people make. It is important to keep several things in mind when considering who is going to pay for LTC:

- Medicare coverage is limited to medically necessary care provided in a nursing home, as well as hospice (end-of-life) care. In addition, it will cover skilled (medically necessary) care in the home. It does not cover custodial care such as nonskilled in-home care, assisted living facilities, or adult day care. My in-laws eventually required 24/7 in-home care, which cost over $100,000 per year. Fortunately, they had saved enough money through proper planning to cover these costs out-of-pocket; not everyone may have this luxury.

---

[1]U.S. Department of Health and Human Services, National Clearinghouse for Long-Term Care Information, www.longtermcare.gov/LTC/Main_Site/Understanding_Long_Term_Care/Basics/Basics.aspx.

- In addition to your care being medically necessary, you must first have been hospitalized for the same condition for at least three days. Medicare will then cover a stay of 20 days, and up to 80 additional days of full to partial coverage based on evaluations made at the facility (this is also subject to deductibles and coinsurance). This coverage is almost always limited to nursing home care, and does not include custodial care (nonskilled care, which typically assists in certain activities of daily living such as dressing, feeding, and so on), and there may be deductibles that you are responsible for.

Myth 3: You Will Be Able to Shelter Your Assets and Let Medicaid Pay Your Bills

Too often, retirees assume Medicaid will pay LTC costs if Medicare does not. While there are ways to plan for Medicaid to pay your bills, this requires you to be impoverished. Some retirees also intend to use personal resources as long as possible and then turn to family or Medicaid. Again, this may or may not be the most suitable way to plan for any LTC needs that may appear in your later years. Here are some facts about Medicaid that you may not be aware of:

- Medicaid is a joint state-federal program, with the majority of the parameters determined by your state. It was designed as a safety net for the truly poor.
- Medicaid's stringent eligibility requirements can be a problem for the at-home spouse if the other spouse needs care in a nursing home or other eligible facility.
- If you have significant pension and/or other retirement income and you need to use a nursing home, a significant portion of your income may have to be used to pay for your care. While there are provisions that allow your spouse to keep a portion of your income if their income is below a certain threshold,[2] this amount called the Minimum Monthly Maintenance Needs Allowance (MMMNA) is almost never enough to maintain the lifestyle to which he or she is accustomed.

---

[2] This threshold amount may vary between states.

- Most states do not cover in-home care or assisted living support, though some exceptions have become available recently. Custodial options, such as adult day care, are almost never covered.
- Using Medicaid raises a number of other issues. Medicaid is not accepted by all LTC facilities, and in other cases there may be a wait for a bed, as Medicaid beds are often limited. Patients on Medicaid may be in a separate part of an LTC facility and almost always get a roommate (not your spouse). Finally, Medicaid does not pay for personal care items such as adult diapers and tissues, or for quality of life activities, such as trips to the mall, the movies, or the hairdresser.

If you still plan to depend on Medicaid to pay your potential LTC expenses, I highly recommend you do three things:

1. Visit the eligible facilities in your area and find out what the facilities and services are like, as well as what the wait is for a Medicaid-eligible bed.
2. Visit your State's Medicaid web site or office. These sites have lots of useful information about the various LTC facilities in your state.
3. Speak with your financial adviser and other professionals.

Myth 4: Your Family Members Will Take Care of You

A generation or two ago, this might have been the case. Today, families are scattered across the country, if not the globe. In addition, the potential caregivers your parents could count on—sisters, wives, and daughters—are often working full-time or have families of their own and cannot take on the care-giving responsibilities you may need.

How You'll Pay

There are three ways to pay for long-term care:

1. *Private Pay.* If you have the money, you can always write the checks to pay for your LTC. I have many clients who have been able to do this through proper planning.

2. *Long-Term Care Insurance (LTCI)*. I also have clients who, though they can afford to use private pay, may elect to offset some of their risk through an LTCI policy. If you can qualify medically because you have good health now, this may be the way to go. I discuss this option in further detail later in the chapter.

3. *Medicaid*. As previously discussed under Common Myths, the state may pay for your care through the Medicaid program if you cannot afford to do so yourself. However, the state can go after assets that you transferred within five years of going into the nursing home and can also try to recover your nursing home costs from your probate estate.

Did You Know?

In terms of planning for retirement, only 22 percent of people ages 45 to 54 and 29 percent of those ages 55 to 64 said that they had given a lot of thought to how they would pay for health care services not covered by Medicare.

Source: HealthAffairs, July 14, 2004.

Examining Which LTC Payment Option Works for You

Before you choose one of the above options for paying for LTC, go through the following process.

Step 1: Assess Your Situation

It is important to assess your lifestyle and family medical history. Some retirees feel that they are unlikely to ever need LTC, and therefore don't buy an LTCI policy. Still, I constantly stress to my clients that it's better to have it and not need it, than to need it and not have it.

Step 2: Address Your Personal Concerns and Responsibilities

Look at your personal concerns and care responsibilities. Many times, for instance, a spouse will try to keep their husband or wife home as long as possible so they do not end up in an LTC facility. I've often observed that the stress of providing this level of care can cause the spouse to eventually need care as well; it may be a burden assumed lovingly, but it's a burden all the same. Still, a good, comprehensive plan will be able to accommodate this situation by providing the necessary resources needed for home health care and other support services; this plan provides the method for taking care of each other with dignity and grace.

Step 3: Review Your Personal and Family Situations

A single or widowed person with limited resources has different concerns about paying for future LTC than a person who has a spouse and a significant pension income. He or she probably has some income from a pension, IRA, or Social Security, but it may not be enough to pay for care in an LTC setting. At the same time, he or she may have too few resources to afford LTCI and too much money to count on Medicaid, at least initially. This is another time when a little advance planning goes a long way, with strategies to stretch those dollars and perhaps find other sources to offset the costs (such as veteran's benefits, if applicable).

Qualifying for VA (Veteran's Administration) Benefits

To qualify for VA benefits, you must meet the following criteria:

1. Served in the active military for a period of 90 consecutive days or more, with at least one day during a period of wartime.
2. Were discharged under other than dishonorable conditions.
3. Are over the age of 65.

There are also some income and asset qualifiers in play here, though they are not as strict as those associated with Medicaid. Be sure to visit an adviser well versed in VA benefit rules if you plan to incorporate these benefits into your financial plan. There are attorneys certified by the VA who will partner with financial advisers to help you in this type of planning. Make sure to shop for the best attorney for your needs.

Step 4: Determine if Spouses Have Unequal Incomes

When two spouses have unequal retirement income (for instance, one spouse has a large pension from his or her company), proper planning is essential to assure that the spouse with the limited income is able to meet his or her own needs in the event that the other spouse ends up in a nursing home. The same applies when a single or widowed person has a home that he or she wishes to pass along to their child. The last part of this chapter has some frequently asked questions (FAQs) and checklists to help you decide what questions to ask and what your needs are, so you can better prepare to meet with your retirement planning professional.

Medicare and Medicaid: Know the Difference!

Medicare, on the one hand, is the Federal health insurance program for Americans aged 65 and older, as well as for certain disabled Americans. It consists of hospital insurance (Part A), which is cost-free, and supplementary medical insurance (Part B), which provides payments for doctors and related services and supplies ordered by the doctor for a premium. Medicare does not cover most nursing home care beyond 100 days, long-term care services in the home (with the exception of skilled care) or prescription drugs (unless you elect for Part D for an additional premium).

Medicaid, on the other hand, provides health care coverage for some low-income people who cannot afford it. It is a federal program in which each state determines eligibility and the scope of health services offered.

Additionally, in the Patient Protection and Affordable Care Act of 2010, a nationwide long-term healthcare plan called the Community Living Assistance Services & Support Act (CLASS) will offer support to those who opt for it. While the details are not concrete it is anticipated that this provision will enable those requiring long-term care to pay a monthly premium for five years. After five years, they will be given a stipend ranging from $50 to $75 a day for their care needs.

Understanding Long-Term Care Insurance

LTCI has many features, benefits, riders and options. Picking the right plan can be a real challenge without the advice of a professional adviser. The most important considerations revolve around LTCI policy basics such as type, duration, and elimination period.

Types of LTCI. There are two main types of LTCI policies: the Daily Benefit Plan and the pool of money. Most people choose the Daily Benefit Plan, which allows you to select an amount your plan will provide on a daily basis. The pool of money plan projects the total monetary need over the course of a given period, and provides a pool of money that can be spent as needed.

Consider the duration. In doing your thorough financial analysis, it is important to consider how long you might wind up needing care. Should you choose a policy that pays a small benefit for a long time, or that pays a large benefit for a shorter period? Since people tend to spend less than five years receiving long-term care, it may make more sense to take a larger daily benefit or pool of money for four or five years, rather than a smaller benefit for the rest of your life as a means of controlling costs/premiums.

Consider the elimination period. The elimination period refers to how long you must be in a facility before your policy begins paying your costs. The longer the elimination period you choose, the lower the cost of the policy will be. Many of my clients take a somewhat longer elimination period so that they can afford a longer total benefit period or larger pool of money, and I tend to recommend an elimination period of at least 90 days. After all, Medicare may pay for at least that much time! If you've got enough money in the bank that you can afford to pay for an additional three months, by all means go with a 6- or even 12-month elimination period and reduce your costs even further. I almost never advise my clients to choose an LTCI policy that pays benefits from the first day of a covered event, as such a policy will have very high premiums.

Don't forget inflation. Unfortunately, LTC costs are rising far faster than inflation, as is the case with almost any type of health insurance and medical care in general. The benefit that seemed so large today may be inadequate in just 5 or 10 years. Many policies will include a simple inflation rider (which adjusts benefits according to the rate of inflation) or a more expensive compound inflation rider (which accounts for the real cost of LTC). I recommend paying extra for an inflation rider when purchasing an LTCI policy.

Reducing Your Costs

Here are a few additional tips for keeping your LTCI costs to a minimum.

Don't wait too long. If you fall into the group who should consider LTC insurance, the biggest mistake you can make is waiting too long to apply for insurance. As you age, two things happen: You become harder to insure and the cost of insurance rises rapidly. At some point, generally in your 80s, LTC insurance is almost impossible to find, let alone qualify for. It's the same as any insurance: If you wait until you need it, it's too late to get it.

Be on the lookout for discounts. Some plans offer discounts if purchased by two or more family members, with special discounts for policies purchased across multiple generations. These savings can be substantial, ranging from 10 to 30 percent over the cost of individual plans. Other methods for reducing the cost of LTCI include purchasing at a younger age—the younger you start the lower the premiums. Increasing the elimination/waiting period is a way to self-insure for what you can afford while still protecting yourself against the potentially catastrophic costs of LTC. It is essential to go with a reputable, highly rated company with a history of holding premiums down so you don't have to worry about premium increases causing your policy to be unaffordable to keep when you need it most.

Reduce the daily benefit. Keep in mind that you'll probably have additional income sources that can offset some of the daily costs of LTC. For instance, let's say you anticipate entering an assisted living facility that costs $6,000 per month, or approximately $200 per day. Well, if you've got a pension, investment income, and Social Security payments amounting to $3,000 per month, you really only need a daily benefit of $100. If there are additional income sources, that number could go down further. There's no sense paying extra for money you won't need!

Meet with a professional who does comprehensive planning. While there are LTC planning techniques to ensure that the community spouse can keep enough assets and income to live comfortably, they require careful planning. For instance, while you can put your assets in trusts or gift them to individuals, there are a number of look-back provisions and potential errors that can invalidate this approach. Likewise, there are a number of trusts and complicated rules that can allow the community spouse to keep a portion of his or her spouse's pension payments and other assets. It is always important to meet with both your financial and legal advisers before repositioning your assets and income. Your tax professional should also be involved to discuss the deductibility of premiums and the benefits of tax-qualified versus nonqualified plans.

What Are My Options with Long-Term Care Insurance?

Long-term care insurance goes far beyond the benefits provided by Medicare or Medicaid. You can choose a plan that covers only nursing home care/dementia facility care, or one that also covers home health care and assisted living facilities. Oftentimes the latter policy will provide additional care options such as adult day care, respite care, home modification, and much more. The following is a quick rundown of the options available to you through LTCI, in order of the level of care provided.

In-Home/Home Health Care   Often people will wish to stay in their own homes long after they begin to need assistance with their Activities of Daily Living (ADLs). This requires the assistance of home health aides, housekeepers, and others. Care received at home can be more expensive than in a nursing home or even an assisted living facility depending on the amount of hours needed. LTC insurance can cover this in tandem with other types of care or as a stand-alone option. While such nonskilled care can cost as little as $10 to $12 an hour, I typically recommend going with an agency that can guarantee that a qualified caregiver will come to your home every day. Such a service can run in the $15 to $17 an hour range.

Home Modifications   You may find yourself in a situation where you do not require an in-home caregiver, but need to modify your home to accommodate the ADLs you can no longer easily perform. For example, the house could be made wheelchair-accessible, the counters could be lowered, or a lift system could be installed on your stairway. Oftentimes the LTC insurer will pay for these modifications, as they are far less expensive than moving you into a facility.

Adult Day Care   In some situations, your family or friends can only provide in-home care for part of the day (usually after work and on weekends). Adult day care facilities provide you with care during the day when your family caregiver cannot.

Respite Care   Even if your family or friends are capable of caring for you for most of the day, sometimes these people need a break. Some LTC insurance policies actually provide for someone to come in and take over for your primary caregiver, or for you to go to a care facility for a period of time.

Assisted Living Care   Many retirees are still largely independent, but just need someone to check in on them and cook their meals. At the same time, the level and/or cost of the care they need exceeds what can be handled at home. Once you get to the point where you require in excess of 40 to 50 hours of in-home care per week, it may make financial sense to look into moving to an assisted living facility.

People often sell their homes and go into a retirement community that is really a continuing care facility. They buy or rent an apartment or patio home and enjoy retirement. When the need arises, they can receive care in their home or move into an apartment in a special area with more extensive care capabilities. Finally, there is often a nursing home attached to the facility if you or your spouse need further care but wish to stay nearby. While costs vary based on the location and quality of the facility, rent typically runs $3,000 to $4,000 a month.

Though LTCI will not cover the independent living portion it will kick in once there is a need for assistance with ADLs.

Nursing Home Care   The level of care provided by an assisted living facility is not unlimited, and you may also eventually require the kind of round-the-clock care that only a nursing home can provide. Some retirees are forced into a nursing home after an injury or other health event that dramatically increases the level of care they need. Remember Sarah, whom I helped to find an assisted living facility a few years back? She recently had a fall and broke her hip, and the X-rays revealed bone cancer that couldn't be treated at her age. Because she was now bedridden and required constant medical attention, she had no choice but to leave her assisted living facility and enter a nursing home.

Nursing home care still tends to be what people think of when they think about LTC. Some costs may be covered by Medicare and Medicaid when and if they provide any benefits. But the real needs and costs—the ones most people need to plan for—are those outside a nursing home. One condition that is commonly associated with nursing homes is Alzheimer's or dementia. However, I have had many clients provide care for a spouse suffering from these conditions at home. It is not easy and an LTC insurance policy that covers Home Health Care could help greatly in covering the cost of home health aides who could greatly relieve the burden of 24/7 care for your loved one. Though those clients providing such care may not think of it as a burden, it can be very hard on them mentally, emotionally, and physically. It is important to understand, as well-meaning and loving as you may be, that you are of no help to either of you if your own health suffers as a result of providing care for a loved one.

If an LTC insurance policy covers care in a nursing home, it almost always covers Alzheimer's/dementia patients. Some assisted living facilities may also have dementia care onsite; this is referred to as a Memory Care Unit.

Should You Buy Long-Term Care Insurance?

Long-term care insurance is like any other financial decision, requiring careful planning and a comprehensive analysis of your financial situation. What are your resources? What is your likelihood of needing care? Are there other resources, like VA benefits, that may become available at some point? I sit down with all my clients to answer these questions, and then look at ways we can reduce the cost of that care.

When conversation turns to LTCI, my clients are inevitably surprised by the affordability and the range of options available to them. Rather than shell out big bucks for the Cadillac of policies, they can pick and choose the services they think they'll want or need. Just as I help my clients determine the needed rate of return on their investments, I also figure out their needed rate of insurance. The goal is always to provide what is needed at a minimal cost.

LTCI can provide the peace of mind of knowing that you'll be taken care of regardless of changes in your family, financial, or health situations. Consider some of the following scenarios:

- You may be operating under the assumption that your family will take care of you, but what if something happens to them?
- What if an unexpected health issue causes you to need more LTC than you anticipated? A broken hip or an Alzheimer's diagnosis can significantly change your care needs.
- Perhaps you've been planning to take care of your spouse at home, but what happens if you wind up needing care yourself?

Purchasing long-term care insurance can eliminate these risks, maintain your independence and freedom of choice, and protect your personal and family assets. If you feel that LTCI is right for you, you should talk to a comprehensive financial planning professional who will take the time to analyze your specific situation and help you find the appropriate policy, not just shuffle you off to an LTCI salesperson looking to sell you more than you need.

What Is the Difference Between Skilled Care And Custodial Care?

Skilled care means care that is medically necessary. People who need skilled care are often suffering from an illness or recovering from an injury. Types of skilled care include physical therapy, speech therapy, help with injections, and the taking of vital signs. Skilled care must be given by a medical professional such as a nurse or therapist.

Custodial care is nonskilled, and typically means assistance with Activities of Daily Living (ADLs). ADLs are considered dressing, transferring, feeding, toileting, and bathing. People who need custodial care may be receiving some skilled care at home but also need help with housekeeping, errands, shopping, and so on. Custodial care is given by a trained paraprofessional, family member, or other caregiver.

Medicare will pay for assistance with ADLs in a setting where it is part of skilled care being provided for qualified services. In other words, there are requirements that need to be met for Medicare to pay for your assistance services. You cannot simply hire a nonqualified assistant and expect Medicare to pay them. They have to be qualified and the assistance you require must be consistent with the plan that you are on.

Frequently Asked Questions

Here are some questions of common concerns I hear from many new clients. Hopefully, these questions and answers can provide a starting point for what you should ask an adviser and then see how their answers compare to other advisers. Keep in mind the goal is not to purchase the Cadillac of LTC policies, it is to first to determine whether you need a policy and if so how to buy only what you need and minimize cost.

Q: How can I guarantee that the premiums will not go up once I purchase an LTC insurance policy?

A: You really cannot, though the exception is insurance companies that offer linked benefits. These are offered through hybrid plans that grow tax deferred in an annuity-type account, with a pool of money available for LTC and/or a death benefit based on the single premium you pay. These policies are typically funded with a single lump sum with monies that can be allocated for just this purpose. Outside of this exception, after the first three to five years, you should plan on 5 to 10 percent increases in your premiums on average per year, for most LTC policies. This does not necessarily mean each and every year your premiums will increase. These increases might not occur but for every three to five years, but they would then potentially go up from 15 to 50 percent. Keep in mind medical care and related expenses typically go up faster than inflation.

Q: Everyone in my family has lived into their 80s and 90s in good health and then died suddenly. Do I need LTC insurance?

A: You may have good genes; however that may not be the only consideration. Sometimes LTC can be required as a result of injury or trauma, and consider this: My father-in-law's father lived well into his 90s and only needed some care at home in the last year of his life, whereas my father-in-law required increasingly extensive care for the last five years of his life due to complications with type-2 diabetes.

Q: I thought Medicare was supposed to cover my health insurance needs now that I am retired, yet you said it rarely covers nursing home care. How can this be? I paid taxes for years!

A: Medicare is intended to pay medical/skilled care costs, not custodial care costs. If you do not need the ongoing, routine services of medical professionals, Medicare does not pay. See the preceding box for an explanation of the difference between skilled and custodial care.

Q: I am planning to transfer my investments and the title to my house to my son and daughter-in-law. Will Medicaid then pay for my LTC if I ever need it?

A: Maybe, maybe not. There are look-back periods that allow assets to be brought back into your asset pool for determining whether you are Medicaid-eligible. Generally, this period is five years, depending on the way you transferred your assets and where the assets went. There are a number of strategies for Medicaid planning, many more than I can cover here, and enough to constitute a book of its own merit. One book I can recommend is *How to Protect Your Family's Assets from Devastating Nursing Home Costs* by Gabriel Heiser.

Additionally, if you give up control of your assets, you may not be able to regain control. This can be a real problem if your condition improves and you no longer need care. There can also be tax consequences to giving up control of your assets, so always make sure to consult with a tax professional.

Q: Is tax-qualified LTC insurance such a big deal?

A: Yes, it can be. If you own a policy that is more than 8 to 10 years old, you may be okay, but newer policies need to meet the TQ criteria to avoid income taxes on benefits.

Last But Not Least

Your quest for financial freedom in retirement is not complete until we take care of your estate-planning needs. For a couple this is assuring that the survivor is able to continue their life in financial freedom and to protect each other through periods of incapacity.

Whether a couple or single, choosing who will take care of you, make health care decisions, manage your assets for your benefit, and ultimately distribute your remaining assets to your heirs is all a part of estate planning. If you don't have a plan, the government has one for you through state intestate laws. This may not be the plan you would prefer, and rest assured it is not designed to reduce state inheritance or federal estate taxes. In fact, it most likely increases costs to your estate, depending on the size, complexity, and number of potential heirs. By the way, if you own real property in other states, your costs just multiplied as you will need multiple attorneys for multiple probates.

In the next chapter I detail the basics of estate planning, with strategies that will help you minimize costs, protect yourself and your family, and help you make sure Uncle Sam is not your biggest beneficiary.

CHAPTER 7

The Basics of Estate Planning

Think it more satisfactory to live richly than die rich.
—Sir Thomas Browne

If you're like many of my clients, you're worried about more than just ensuring that your assets will help create a comfortable retirement. You may also be looking ahead to the legacy you leave to your children and grandchildren after you've passed away.

As I discussed in Chapter 3, retirement planning changed during the baby boom generation. The decline in private pension plans and the subsequent introduction of IRAs and 401(k)s meant that people were now responsible for their own retirement income streams. If you want to have income in retirement, you have to put money away yourself.

This shift also drove a sea change in estate planning. Where before retirees could simply rely on their pension and Social Security for income and pass along their savings to their children, people today have saved money out of necessity. Your savings, in other words, are no longer a Rainy Day Fund that can simply be passed along to your kids—they are the foundation of your retirement plan. Combined with the fact that many retirees have already paid to put their children through college, it's increasingly common for people to spend down the majority of their savings during their retirement, leaving less to pass along to their heirs.

Of course, that's not to say that estate planning has become any less important. Even if you're not inclined to make sacrifices in order to pass money along to your children, you still want to have a plan for your money, and nobody wants to let their savings go to the government rather than to their children. Many of you probably wonder if it is possible to enjoy retirement to the fullest, have personal and financial matters taken care of in case of incapacitation, and still leave a legacy for your loved ones without sacrificing your own lifestyle. The answer is yes! With careful planning and professional assistance, it is possible to reduce taxes and expenses, maximize the asset value for you and your heirs, minimize the amount of time it takes to disburse those assets to loved ones, and protect your own and your loved ones privacy. As I say to my clients the best plan is the one that, God forbid, should you die tomorrow it will serve your wishes and should you, God willing, live to 100, it will still serve your needs.

Why Estate Planning?

Estate planning is an important and powerful tool because it:

- Provides peace of mind that you will have a comfortable, worry-free retirement for you and your spouse.
- Maintains control while you are alive and after you die.
- Helps you plan for incapacity.
- Ensures that any business you leave behind transitions smoothly according to your goals.
- Reduces income taxes for you and your spouse during your lifetime and for your heirs after you die.
- Reduces and, in many cases, eliminates estate and inheritance taxes.
- Establishes specific instructions for taking care of dependents after you die and, in some cases, attaches conditions to how your heirs can use their inheritance.
- Provides a legacy for your heirs.

- Releases your assets to your beneficiaries quickly and with minimal expense by avoiding probate.
- Can provide for a charitable cause with potential tax benefits during your lifetime.
- Protects your valuable property and assets during your lifetime and for generations to come.
- Is a private matter and allows you to handle your assets at your discretion.

Unfortunately, many of my clients underestimate the importance of meeting with an estate planner to ensure that these goals are achieved. Some people are under the impression that estate planning is a simple matter of working with a lawyer to draw up a will. Such an attitude is a one-way ticket to probate court, which can undermine your efforts to leave a legacy for your loved ones. Indeed, by relying on a traditional "I love you" will that simply leaves everything to your surviving spouse and heirs, you will likely miss out on all the benefits that can be gained through proper estate planning.

Did You Know?

In 2000, The American Association of Retired Persons (AARP) reported that only 18 percent of people with incomes of $25,000 or less had a trust, while 53 percent of seniors with moderate and higher incomes had a trust. Don't read too much into this statistic though—when deciding whether or not to get a trust, the primary determinant should be your net worth, not your retirement income.

The survey also indicated that only 38 percent of people over the age of 50 had both a will and a power of attorney. Another 20 percent of this age group had a will but no power of attorney. This means that 42 percent of people over the age of 50 have no plan to deal with their estate.

Source: Where There is a Will... , April 2000, http://assets.aarp.org/rgcenter/econ/will.pdf.

Problematic Probate

In simple terms, probate is the legal process of proving the validity of your will and providing for the orderly distribution of your worldly goods according to the instructions in the will and any applicable state laws. This process involves disclosing and accounting for your assets in a court-supervised environment, paying your creditors, and disbursing the remainder of your assets to your beneficiaries.

Unfortunately, probate is anything but simple. History is littered with tales of endless probate proceedings that outlive the original heirs—famously, Marilyn Monroe's estate spent 18 years in probate court! There are a number of reasons why it's in your best interests to avoid probate:

- The process can easily take 12 months or more—one probate case in Tennessee is currently entering its ninth year, with no end in sight.
- There's no privacy—probate is a matter of public record, so every last detail about your estate and your will is revealed and open to the public. Anyone so inclined can walk into the courthouse and view your probate records.
- The executor or personal representative who handles your estate may have significant expenses. One famous case involving a $17 million estate wound up racking up nearly $1.5 million in attorney's fees and executor's commissions.
- Probate also involves such expenses as attorney, accounting, and appraisal fees. Considered a cash cow for attorneys, the AARP estimates that of the $2 billion spent annually on probate, nearly $1.5 billion of that goes to attorney's fees.
- As probate is a forum for dispute, it opens up your estate to sometimes frivolous claims from creditors and disgruntled heirs, which can be used as leverage to negotiate settlements from legitimate heirs.
- If you were to own real property in multiple states, you would be subject to multiple probates of your entire estate in each of those states. Needless to say, the court fees and taxes are multiplied in this instance.
- Avoids agonizing conservatorship hearings should you become incompetent.

For more information on the probate process, see Exhibit 7.1.

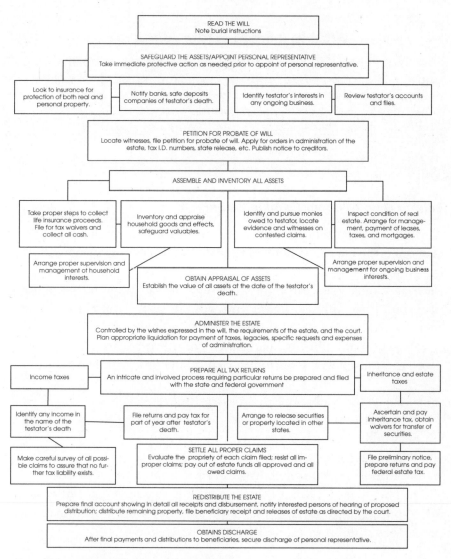

READ THE WILL
Note burial instructions

SAFEGUARD THE ASSETS/APPOINT PERSONAL REPRESENTATIVE
Take immediate protective action as needed prior to appoint of personal representative.

Look to insurance for protection of both real and personal property.

Notify banks, safe deposits companies of testator's death.

Identify testator's interests in any ongoing business.

Review testator's accounts and files.

PETITION FOR PROBATE OF WILL
Locate witnesses, file petition for probate of will. Apply for orders in administration of the estate, tax I.D. numbers, state release, etc. Publish notice to creditors.

ASSEMBLE AND INVENTORY ALL ASSETS

Take proper steps to collect life insurance proceeds. File for tax waivers and collect all cash.

Inventory and appraise household goods and effects, safeguard valuables.

Identify and pursue monies owed to testator, locate evidence and witnesses on contested claims.

Inspect condition of real estate. Arrange for management, payment of leases, taxes, and mortgages.

Arrange proper supervision and management of household interests.

OBTAIN APPRAISAL OF ASSETS
Establish the value of all assets at the date of the testator's death.

Arrange proper supervision and management for ongoing business interests.

ADMINISTER THE ESTATE
Controlled by the wishes expressed in the will, the requirements of the estate, and the court. Plan appropriate liquidation for payment of taxes, legacies, specific requests and expenses of administration.

Income taxes

PREPARE ALL TAX RETURNS
An intricate and involved process requiring particular returns be prepared and filed with the state and federal government

Inheritance and estate taxes

Identify any income in the name of the testator's death

File returns and pay tax for part of year after testator's death.

Arrange to release securities or property located in other states.

Ascertain and pay inheritance tax, obtain waivers for transfer of securities.

Make careful survey of all possible claims to assure that no further tax liability exists.

SETTLE ALL PROPER CLAIMS
Evaluate the propriety of each claim filed; resist all improper claims; pay out of estate funds all approved and all owed claims.

File preliminary notice, prepare returns and pay federal estate tax.

REDISTRIBUTE THE ESTATE
Prepare final account showing in detail all receipts and disbursement, notify interested persons of hearing of proposed distribution; distribute remaining property, file beneficiary receipt and releases of estate as directed by the court.

OBTAINS DISCHARGE
After final payments and distributions to beneficiaries, secure discharge of personal representative.

Exhibit 7.1   Getting through Probate

If your goal is to disburse your assets in a speedy, private, and cost-effective manner, then probate court is clearly the last place you want to end up. How do estates end up there, and how can you avoid it?

What Is a Small Estate Affidavit?

A Small Estate Affidavit is a procedure allowed under small estate laws that enable heirs to obtain property from an estate without probate, or with shorter probate proceedings. These procedures tend to minimize both cost and time and can be used whether there is a will or not. Typically these are used for estates valued at less than $25,000, though this amount can vary between states.

Relying On a Will: Your Ticket to Probate

A will is simply a set of instructions on how to distribute your property once the state has determined that you truly own what is listed in the will. While it is typically sufficient to pass along your assets, it invariably must pass through probate court, a messy and expensive proposition. A will also leaves you without any privacy, as all documents are made known in probate court and become public record.

People today tend to lead more complicated lives that require more than just a will. Consider looking beyond a will if you have:

- Real estate, especially across multiple states.
- A desire to control assets to protect your family.
- A desire for privacy.
- A need for flexibility.
- A preference for avoiding delays.
- The goal of leaving the most money to your heirs rather than paying potentially exorbitant attorney's fees, administrative fees, and other related probate expenses.

In particular, probate cases involving real estate in multiple states illustrate the importance of going beyond a will. For example, let's say you owned a condo in Florida in addition to your home in Tennessee. Upon your death, your family would be forced to open probate in both states on your entire estate, doubling the cost of an already expensive process.

Real estate holdings also tend to be problematic for other reasons. In one case, a man with four childrepan passed away, leaving them to attempt to divide up a parcel of land he'd owned. Several years of bickering in probate court resolved nothing, and when they eventually died, each of their children was left with a claim to a tiny fraction of the original land. The accumulated legal costs of the process have far exceeded the value of the property.

Can You Avoid Probate?

I've had people come into my office and tell me that their attorney had advised them that they could avoid probate simply by adding their children to their deed and utilizing Payable on Death (POD) or Transfer on Death (TOD) to transfer their other assets. However, in such an instance, you may not be getting the whole story.

Most spouses own property and non-retirement assets through a form of joint ownership known as Joint Tenants with Rights of Survivorship. Although this avoids probate, there are various pitfalls. For instance, the death of one of the joint tenants increases the size of the surviving tenant's estate, potentially creating additional tax liability (see the sidebar "One Pitfall of Joint Tenancy"). If you add your child (or any nonspouse) to your deed, there are other complications, including the potential for your child's creditors making claims to that asset. Additionally, there may be gift tax liability in some states.

There also could be higher capital gains taxes when your child eventually sells the house. If you gift your house or other asset to your children while you're alive they take your cost basis for the asset. In other words, for capital gains tax purposes, they use the amount that you paid. If you paid $100,000 for the house and transferred it to your children via gifting and they sold it for $400,000 they would pay a capital gains tax on the $300,000 appreciation. If they inherit the house instead they would receive a stepped-up cost basis as of your date of death. If the property was worth $400,000 at the time of your death and they sold it for that amount they would not pay any capital gains tax on that asset. Leaving the property in a will or a trust avoids both gift taxes and capital gains taxes.

Payable on Death is a common practice that allows you to designate a beneficiary to receive a given asset upon your death. While POD can be beneficial in very narrow applications, there are better ways to accomplish your goals that will give you many more options and more protection. For instance, neither PODs nor TODs provide contingencies if the beneficiary dies or becomes incapacitated.

One Pitfall of Joint Tenancy

Let's say you live in Tennessee, where the inheritance tax exemption is $1 million, and have joint ownership of a $2 million estate with your spouse. If your spouse dies with only an "I love you" will, his or her share of the assets will transfer to you, making you the sole owner of the $2 million estate. Upon your death, then, half of your total estate (the value beyond $1 million) will be subjected to the state and federal inheritance taxes before passing to your heirs, costing them about $80,000 in taxes. Had you used a Credit Shelter Trust (as I explain later in this chapter), your spouse's inheritance tax exemption would have been preserved and you would have avoided the inheritance tax altogether. By spending less than $2,000 on this kind of planning, you could have saved your heirs $80,000.

Note: The Federal Estate tax was temporarily lifted for 2010. Under current law Federal Estate taxes will revert to $1 million in 2011; this means that upon your death your estate will be taxed at a 55 percent rate if the value is over $1 million.

All About Trusts

When it comes to estate planning, I almost always advise my clients to set up a trust. A trust is a private legal entity whereas a will is a public document that can be contested in probate court by creditors and angry relatives.

The following terms and definitions may be helpful in understanding the parties to a trust:

- The **Trustor** is the person who sets up the trust (usually with the help of an attorney) and funds the trust.
- The **Trustee** is put in charge of the trust's assets by the Trustor. The trustee is usually also the Trustor. (For couples, typically both people are Trustors and Trustees.)
- The **Successor Trustee** (usually a family member) takes control of the trust upon the Trustee's death or incapacitation.

Upon taking control, the successor trustee's responsibility is first to manage the trust assets for the Trustee through a period of incapacity and for the benefit of the Primary Beneficiary (many times this is the Trustor/Trustee). The Trustees and Successor Trustees have a fiduciary responsibility to the beneficiaries. This is a legal obligation to act in the best interest of the beneficiaries, putting their interest ahead of the Trustees' own. After the death of the Trustor(s)/Trustee(s) the successor trustee is obligated to continue to manage and eventually to distribute the assets to the beneficiaries as dictated by the trust.

- The **Primary Beneficiary List** starts with the Trustor(s) (as they get the benefit of the assets while they're alive), followed by the Trustor's chosen heirs—children, grandchildren, charities, and so on.

The Five Essential Documents

There are numerous types of trusts that I will briefly describe later in this chapter that may be used. However, the following five documents form the foundation of a sound estate for most of my clients.

Revocable Living Trust (RLT)

The revocable living trust is the core document that I recommend for the majority of my clients. They are very flexible, relatively uncomplicated, inexpensive to set up, and easy to dissolve or change.

Revocable living trusts are simply trusts that can be revoked or changed, and which take effect while you are still alive. You can be your own trustee, allowing you to control how the money, property, and other assets are managed, used, and/or invested.

The best advice I can give you with any revocable trust is to make sure you fund it; that is, make sure the assets that are going into the trust actually get there. Otherwise it will be empty, and what good is a safe if you leave your valuables outside of it? To fund your trust, the title to each asset must be retitled. Instead of your home being held in the names "John and Mary Smith," part of setting up the trust involves changing the deed to read "John and Mary Smith, Trustees of the John and Mary Smith Revocable Living Trust." By actually putting the assets into the trust, your assets transfer directly to the named beneficiary, thereby avoiding probate. You are essentially pre-probating your estate.

This type of trust also allows you to:

- Name the trustees (including yourself or both you and your spouse).
- Name your successor trustees.
- Name your beneficiaries.
- Control the assets listed in the trust.
- Take assets out and put them in.
- Completely revoke the trust, as its name implies.
- Change the trust during your lifetime.

Revocable trusts also do something that is very valuable: they avoid some of the problems associated with personal incapacitation. For instance, in the case that you were deemed incompetent or unable to care for yourself—perhaps due to Alzheimer's, a stroke, or some other unfortunate medical problem—your assets cannot then be managed without a court-appointed representative to act on your behalf. This takes time and costs money. Your spouse or other family member would most likely be the one going to court and absorbing that expense. The process typically costs thousands of dollars and can take upwards of six months to complete depending on your state and attorney. Subsequently, any fighting and bickering between family members about the stipulations of the will may add to the expense and the delay. If you own an asset as a joint tenant with rights of survivorship (JWTROS), the entire asset is likewise tied up if one owner is deemed unable to make a decision to sell.

By contrast, with the revocable living trust you have already preselected who will be in charge of your assets if you become incapacitated. The assets are thus protected from living probate or conservatorship actions, as you have already named who you want to be in charge of the assets in case of this event. As long as one trustee is able to act, he or she can act on behalf of all of the trustees.

The revocable trust dictates your wishes as trustor and sets forth all the language and instructions on what will happen at given times and in certain circumstances. It can provide for management of the assets long after your death. For example, I have had many clients concerned about leaving money outright to certain of their children for fear they would squander the money and then look to their siblings for help. The solution many times is to leave the irresponsible child's share in trust to be managed either by family or an independent trustee, or possibly both as co-trustees. The trustee(s) then provide for the financial needs of the child and assure that the child will be cared for, thus protecting them from themselves. You can also include provisions if you have children with special needs that provide them with supplemental assistance while still allowing them to qualify for aid from public assistance programs.

Pour-Over Will

A pour-over will is also known as your Last Will and Testament. The term "pour over" refers to the fact that this document pours over any assets in the estate that were not put in the trust. The language in the will leaves all of these assets to the trust, acting as a safety net of sorts. The downside is that the assets transferred by the will have to first pass through probate. Thus, although it is important to have a pour-over will, ideally you will never have to use it.

Other Trust Provisions for Asset Management

Trusts can have various provisions for how the assets are to be used long after your death. These provisions are very helpful in cases where there are minor children or adult children that may not be fiscally responsible. Here are some examples:

Spendthrift clause—Protects trust assets from attachment by any beneficiary's creditors.

Discretionary distributions—The trustee may be limited to distributing income or principal for specific purposes such as education or medical needs.

Income only—Some beneficiaries could be limited to receiving just the income from the trust without dipping into the principal. In some cases, their right to access the principal could be withheld until they reach a certain age, typically one-third of the principal at age 25, one-half of the remaining principal at 30, and the remaining balance at 35.

I have recently had first-hand experience in the importance of pour-over wills. One example, Rachel, a client of mine, passed away some years ago. A couple of years after she passed, a check arrived in the mail made out to Rachel. The check contained the proceeds from the life insurance policy of a distant aunt. Without a pour-over will, the benefits of this policy would have been distributed according to state law, and counter to Rachel's wishes. Because she had a pour-over will, however, the payout passed into Rachel's trust, and was thereby distributed to her heirs according to her wishes. As you can see, even with diligent efforts on my part in funding the trust at its creation and regular reviews to ensure Rachel's assets were titled properly to her trust, exceptions can arise beyond our control.

General Durable Power of Attorney

This document operates outside of the trust. Its primary purpose is to handle financial and business matters that do not necessarily relate directly to the trust, such as IRAs, pensions, or other retirement accounts. These types of retirement accounts may not be titled in the name of the trust, as they would trigger a taxable event.

The following is an example to help you understand the importance of this document. A couple sets up a trust and names each other as co-trustees. The husband becomes incapacitated, and although the wife can continue to manage the assets in the trust, she cannot access his retirement accounts. If these accounts made up a considerable portion of their assets, this could create a financial hardship for the couple.

The wife would have to hire an attorney and petition the probate court to appoint her as conservator of her husband. In many states, this could take between three to six months and cost in the range of $3,000. Additionally, she would have to report to the court how the money is used, requiring her to use both an attorney and an accountant to help her appropriately file the mandatory annual court paperwork. This added expense could have been avoided by having a General Durable Power of Attorney!

Power of Attorney for Health Care

This document allows you to appoint someone to make health care decisions on your behalf in the event that you are incapacitated. If you don't have this document, a court can appoint a conservator for you who may not fully understand your wishes. This document can be obtained at any hospital or online. Unlike most of the documents listed here, you can usually fill this document out yourself, without the aid of an attorney. Many estate-planning attorneys and hospitals provide this document at no cost.

Living Will

Living wills—which attained some national exposure during the Terri Schiavo controversy—give instructions regarding the use of so-called "life-sustaining measures" in the event that your attending physician has determined that your condition is terminal. You can add requests concerning respirators, intravenous feeding, and organ donation. Although this document is considered optional, I highly recommend that you state these wishes in writing to save your family the hardship that attends such an event. This document is also available at hospitals, and many attorneys include this as a foundational document at no cost.

Lightning Round: Other Types of Trusts

While the revocable living trust tends to be my foundation trust that I recommend for the majority of my clients, your personal circumstances may call for additional planning, especially when you face potential estate taxes. The following is a quick rundown of some common trusts. As always, it's important to consult with an estate planner when attempting to set up a trust.

Credit Shelter Trusts, also known as Family Trusts or A-B Trusts, are for couples whose combined assets exceed the unified credit exemption from the estate and gift taxes. Estate tax rates are quite onerous and apply to all of the assets you own at the time of your death. The maximum federal estate tax rate for 2011 will be 35 percent under the sunset provision of the Economic Growth and Tax Relief Reconciliation Act of 2001 (EGTRRA), and when combined with state inheritance taxes, can exceed 50 percent depending on the state. The unified credit exemption is the amount you can pass along to your children tax-free without incurring an estate tax liability. Because of the tremendous tax benefits of the unified credit exemption, I use this whenever I set up a Revocable Living Trust for a married couple. This type of trust allows you to preserve your unified credit exemption when you die and pass your estate on to your spouse, thereby passing twice the assets to your children tax-free.

Using the 2011 exemption amounts, you and your spouse could each pass on to your children $1 million free from estate tax ($2 million total) utilizing a credit shelter trust strategy. It is important to note that the estate and gift tax exemptions are constantly in flux (see Exhibit 7.2 for the prognosis for 2009 to 2011, based on current law). Though the unified credit has been unlimited for 2010, in the absence of Congressional action it will drop back down to $1 million in 2011.[1] So it is important to make sure your estate-planning documents are kept up to date in light of any changes.

Qualified Terminable Interest Property (Q-TIP) Trusts are for people who get remarried and wish to leave their assets to the children from the first marriage. They are also used by those who wish to protect their assets in the event that their spouse remarries after their death. A Q-TIP trust provides your spouse with the full use of your assets including any income, but ensures that the principal will go to your children upon your death.

Charitable Remainder Trusts (CRTs) allow you to leave part or all of your estate to a qualifying charitable institution. With a CRT, you

---

[1] While current law calls for the estate tax exemption to drop to $1 million in 2013, for 2011 and 2012 the exemption has been raised to $5 million and this has again been unified with the lifetime gift exclusion. The federal estate tax rate is set at 35 percent for 2011 and 2012. This opens up some interesting options for large estates, wherein they could gift $5 million ($10 million for couples) this year or next, and if the estate and gift tax exemptions do sunset under current law they will have avoided a very large tax (55 percent).

Exhibit 7.2 The Estate Tax Credit

Year	Estate Tax Exemption	Minimum Tax Rates
2009	$3.5 million	45%
2010	Unlimited	35% (gift tax only)
2011	$5 million	35%
2012	$5 million	35%
2013	$1 million	55%

Note that the gift tax exemption is set at $1 million, though there has been support on Capitol Hill to raise it to $3.5 million permanently.

get to keep the income from your assets while you're alive, and take a large tax deduction. CRTs have other applications that, when combined with other strategies, can provide tax-advantaged income and turn more assets subject to estate taxes into tax-free money for heirs.

Family Foundations are intended as a very advanced planning strategy for estates that tend to be $5 million or greater. If you have an estate this large, I would first like to congratulate you; and second, I would like to recommend that you go directly to a certified professional for planning and management. With such a large estate, planning for you is even more important, and can provide even greater benefits—you have much more at stake! Without proper planning, taxes could decimate your estate.

Irrevocable Trusts are trusts that cannot be canceled. The most common type is the Irrevocable Life Insurance Trust (ILIT), which can be used to pass life insurance proceeds to beneficiaries (outside your estate) free from income, inheritance, and estate taxes. In addition to passing a tax-free legacy to your children, this can also be used to provide liquidity to the children to pay estate taxes on illiquid assets. Irrevocable trusts can also be used for asset protection and Medicaid planning.

Family Limited Partnerships are created for business purposes, such as managing stocks or taking care of a farm. Assets placed in a Family Limited Partnership enjoy a discount for estate tax purposes, though this discount is presently under scrutiny by the IRS. Family Limited Partnerships are primarily used for asset protection policies.

Please note that this is only a brief overview of these additional trusts.

Whom Should I Name as Trustee?

When setting up a trust, one of the biggest decisions you have to make is who to name as your trustee. I like to tell my clients to ask themselves: "Who do I want handling my money and my business affairs in case I become incapacitated? If I have to rely on someone else, do I totally trust them to make smart decisions, motivated solely by what is best for me, my spouse, and my family?" In most cases married couples name each other first; however, they also need to name successor trustees in the event that neither of them can serve due to disability or death.

With this in mind, make sure the person is:

- Someone you trust completely to act in your best interests and those of your heirs. In fact, a trustee is held to a fiduciary legal standard, meaning that he or she is legally obligated to work in your best interests.
- Someone who is willing to accept the responsibilities of a trustee. This person will have to make a substantial time investment, as well as deal with relatives, banks, and possibly attorneys and others.
- Someone who is physically able to handle the job. While the trustee(s) can live out of state, closer is often better.
- Someone with the business acumen and good judgment for the position. This need not be someone who works in the financial sector, just someone who has the good judgment to hire experts to assist him or her when necessary.

You may consider appointing a financial institution as your trustee if your trust is complicated and/or no one you trust is available or willing to do the job. Also remember that you can always have multiple people act as trustees together or with a corporate trustee. This can ensure a better balance or help assure you that the best job possible will be done.

I also recommend appointing an investment adviser to the trust to act in avoiding conflicts of interest and to help minimize costs. Ideally, they would also share your investment philosophy.

The Value of Real Professionals: Finding the Right Certified Expert

While estate planning has a lot to do with personal preferences, it also involves decisions about hard-earned assets that you do not want to lose. For making these kinds of decisions, it's absolutely crucial to find the best certified or accredited estate-planning expert for you.

Do not think that software or a how-to book can ever equate to the value of consulting with real professionals who understand the ins and outs of estate planning. I once had a gentleman come into my office seeking information on estate planning. He already had a trust that he'd set up for the purposes of avoiding probate and thereby maintain both privacy and control of his assets. There was just one problem: He created the trust himself.

Looking at his do-it-yourself trust, it was quickly apparent that it did not meet his needs. I explained that he'd set up a testamentary trust, which will not get funded or go into effect until his death. Unfortunately for him, this meant that it would have to go through probate first—the very thing he was trying to avoid!

It's also important to make sure you find a specialist. Just as you would never settle for a general practitioner to take care of a rare medical condition, it is likewise important to find someone who specializes specifically in estate planning.

Once you have a basic idea of what you want to accomplish with your assets, you should consult an estate-planning attorney. I would recommend you start your search by looking for a member of the National Association of Estate Planners and Counsels at NAEPC. org. Another good resource for finding an estate-planning attorney in your area is TheEstatePlan.com, or the American Academy of Estate Planning Attorneys. These resources are good for finding an attorney, a tax adviser with estate-planning experience, or a financial adviser who is accredited for estate planning. They can provide the most comprehensive advice, depth of knowledge, and expertise to determine the optimum estate-planning strategies.

While I myself am an accredited estate planner (AEP), I always help my clients find an estate-planning attorney, and work closely with that attorney to draw up the necessary documents. For more information on living trusts, I recommend Henry Abts's books, which can be found at any bookstore. Additional information can also be found at the TheEstatePlan.com.

Elvis Presley's Estate

One of the most famous examples of a poorly implemented estate plan was Elvis'. His estate lost about 73 percent of its value to estate taxes and probate fees. Celebrities, like the rest of us, need a well-thought-out estate plan. However, there was no stopping the King—he actually has earned more money since his death than when he was alive!

Here are a few things to keep in mind when seeking an estate planner:

- Shop around. Price can vary, and a higher price does not necessarily mean that you are getting better advice.
- Be on the lookout for living trust mills that deliver cookie-cutter documents that do nothing to address individual needs, typically do not provide a face-to-face consultation with an estate-planning attorney, and may not hold up if challenged in court. Such operations have even been known to provide documents that aren't valid for your state of residence!
- Get the price up front, in writing, before entering into an arrangement for setting up your trust.
- Be wary of attorneys or advisers that do not provide you with a free initial consultation.
- Do not assume that everything an expert tells you is right for you. There is nothing wrong with getting a second opinion or doing research so you can better understand what you are doing.
- Make sure your expert takes the time to do his or her due diligence, as well as explain any concepts that might confuse you.

As a final note, it's important to keep in mind that estate planning must be considered as part and parcel of your overall retirement planning strategy, not as a separate issue. Here's an example:

Nicholas came to me with $2.4 million in total assets, $800,000 of which was in a traditional IRA. By setting up a credit shelter trust for him and his wife, we were able to ensure that he could pass $2 million along to his heirs, inheritance and estate tax-free.

We weren't done, though! Rather than settle for subjecting the additional $400,000 to the federal estate tax, we instead converted the traditional IRA to a Roth IRA, which allowed us to pay the income tax on the IRA assets (about $250,000) up front. Combined with some gifting, we were able to get the total value of the estate under $2 million. The result was that we not only avoided the federal estate tax and state inheritance taxes altogether, but also guaranteed that the money in the IRA subject to income taxes would not also be subject to state and inheritance taxes. This avoided what would have resulted in triple taxation of the IRA! Nicholas did not intend to use the money from his IRA account to maintain his lifestyle and expected the money to go to his children—this was a sound investment strategy.

As you can see, estate-planning strategies go hand-in-hand with general financial planning, which makes it all the more important to find people whose expertise encompasses both fields.

Frequently Asked Questions

As in the previous chapter I thought it might be helpful to provide common questions new clients ask. I have had new clients tell me they don't even know what to ask, let alone the answers. Hopefully this will give you a starting point and to help you find good advisers.

Q: What happens if I die without a will or a trust?
A: Dying without a will or other binding document is called "intestacy." The court will appoint a personal representative to serve as the administrator to take care of what you have left behind in terms of assets, expenses, and taxes. Your estate will be subject to probate, which may take even longer because you did not provide any specific instructions through a will or trust on how to disburse your assets and pay your bills and taxes. Your assets are distributed to your next-of-kin based on state law, and the rules vary from state to state. If the court does not find any legal heirs, your property could

go to the government. In the end, you do yourself and your heirs a real disservice by not having any estate plan in place.

Q: What are some of the reasons people set up trusts?

A: People set up trusts in order to:

- Maintain control over their assets during their lifetime and after they die.
- Provide lifetime care for a disabled relative or heir.
- Minimize inheritance and estate taxes.
- Leave assets to children from a former marriage.
- Protect assets if your spouse remarries after your death.
- Avoid probate and protect assets from conservatorship.
- Ensure their privacy and keep prying eyes out of their affairs.

Q: Can I set up my own trust(s)?

A: Yes, you can. However, these are legal documents and it is easy to miss something, leave vital information out, or even set up the wrong kind of trust altogether. It is far better to utilize certified professional advisers in this process. Better to spend a little to save a lot than be penny-wise and pound-foolish.

Q: What could happen if there is something wrong with how my trust was set up?

A: There are a variety of scenarios that could put your assets at risk or cause you or your heirs a number of headaches. For instance, you could potentially subject your estate to unnecessary taxes, inadvertently disinherit an heir, or unintentionally give assets to an heir you don't like. Ideally, work with an accredited estate planner/financial planner who works with a board-certified estate-planning attorney.

Q: What happens if I fail to re-title my assets into the trust?

A: This is also known as funding your trust. If you fail to do so, it will have to be funded at your death through probate, which will cause unnecessary cost and delay the distribution of your assets.

Q: How much does it cost to have an attorney set up a trust?

A: The cost depends on the type of trust and the area in which you live. For the five foundation documents I recommend, the cost can range from $1,500 to $2,500 on the low end, to $5,000 to $10,000 on the high end. This is why it's important to shop around—the difference in price may have little to do with the qualifications of the estate-planning attorney or the quality of the documents.

Q: I already have a will and my attorney tells me that my estate is not large enough to need a trust. Is this true?

A: It is quite possible that you do not need a trust. However, it is best to review your options with an accredited estate planner and/or a board certified estate-planning attorney. It doesn't cost anything to get a second opinion—you have everything to gain and nothing to lose.

Q: We plan to move to another state next year. Do we need to change our will or trust provisions?

A: Depending on the laws of your new home state, you may need to change your will, and if you have power of attorney documents, they may need to be replaced. The trust should be okay, but it would be a good idea to have it reviewed to make sure it's properly funded. Your current accredited estate planner/financial planner and board-certified estate-planning attorney should be able to refer a qualified attorney in your new home state.

Remember: The cost of creating and administering a trust depends on the type and duration of the trust. Legal fees are based on the consultation, planning, and preparation time. Before hiring a lawyer, always discuss fees and try to arrange a written fee agreement. A corporate trustee's fee may be tied to the size and complexity of the trust estate, though by having a separate, independent investment adviser you should be able to minimize the fees.

Estate Planning Checklist

The following checklist will only take a few minutes to fill out, but will go a long way toward helping you determine how much work you need to do in formulating an estate-planning strategy.

Estate Planning Checklist

	Yes/Date	No
Do you have a will?		
Do you have a revocable living trust?		
Is your revocable living trust funded?		
Do you have life insurance?		
Is your life insurance in an ILIT?		
Do you plan to gift assets to charity?		
Have you established a CRT?		
Do you have durable/medical powers of attorney?		
Do you have a safe deposit box?		
Can your trustee(s) and executor(s) access your safe deposit box?		
Do you have an inventory of what is in your safe deposit box?		
Have you ensured your trustee(s) and executor(s) are able and willing to perform their tasks?		
Have you set up POD accounts?		
Are the primary and secondary beneficiaries of your life insurance and retirement accounts current?		
Do you own property in another state?		
Do you have disabled heirs that require care?		
Do you want to leave assets to children from a previous marriage?		

Where to Go from Here

There are many great resources and organizations to help you find qualified advisors in your area. Ed Slott's website www.irahelp.com is a great resource. Henry Abts company The Estate Plan and its web site www.theestateplan.com is another. The National Association of Estate Planners and Councils website www.naepc.org is another good resource for qualified estate planners and estate planning attorneys. The Society of Financial Service Professional (www.financialpro.org) is a good resource for qualified financial advisors.

For more help, you can also go to my website www.hankparrott .com for additional links. Bottom line, you will need a team of advisers willing to work together putting your best interest first. You now have the tools and the knowledge to help you on your journey to financial freedom in retirement.

A

Confidential Lifestyle Questionnaire

Estate & Financial
Strategies, Inc.
Registered Investment Advisor

Confidential Lifestyle Questionnaire

Name: _____

Address: _____

_____

Day Phone: _____ Cell Phone: _____

E-mail: _____ May we contact you via e-mail?
Yes ❑   No ❑ (We will not share your e-mail address with anyone)

Birthday (Client): _____ Birthday (Spouse): _____

Family Members:

<u>Children (Name)</u>	<u>Age</u>	<u># of Grandchildren (if any)</u>
_____	_____	_____
_____	_____	_____
_____	_____	_____
_____	_____	_____
_____	_____	_____
_____	_____	_____

How would you like to see your assets distributed after your death?
In lump sums? Over time as some type of payment program?

Who would you like to supervise the distribution of your assets? Is
that person(s) emotionally and financially capable?

The answers you provide to the following questions will help us to determine whether or not we think there is a fit between us. In our experience, successful financial planning can only take place if we share a similar philosophy about financial planning, and if we both agree that we can work together.

	Name	Satisfaction Level (10 is best)

1. Do you currently work with a(n):

    a. Financial Adviser ❏ _____   1 2 3 4 5 6 7 8 9 10

    b. Investment Adviser ❏ _____   1 2 3 4 5 6 7 8 9 10

    c. Estate Planner ❏ _____   1 2 3 4 5 6 7 8 9 10

    d. CPA ❏ _____   1 2 3 4 5 6 7 8 9 10

    e. Other (please specify) _____   1 2 3 4 5 6 7 8 9 10

2. What stage are you at in your career? (check all that apply):

    a. Mid-career   ❏

    b. Nearing retirement   ❏

    c. Semi-retired   ❏

    d. Retired   ❏

    e. Not planning to retire   ❏

3. Do you own and operate your own business or professional practice?

    Yes ❏   No ❏

If yes, tell me about it. If no, please tell me about your career.

4. Do you have an estate plan? Yes ❏   No ❏ Are you satisfied with it? Why or why not? Are charities involved, and if so, which ones? Why them?

5. Do you ever lose sleep worrying about money? If so, what are those concerns?

6. If you won the lottery and money was no longer a concern, how would your life change?

7. If you only had five years to live, how would your life change?

8. If you died tomorrow, what regrets would you have of things not done in your life?

9. Where you spend your time and your money is where your heart is: What is important to you?

10. How much money would you need to not worry about money? Are you there now?

11. What do you hope to accomplish as a result of our meeting together?

What's Important About Money to You?

_____

_____

_____

_____

_____

_____

_____

_____

_____

_____

_____

_____

_____

_____

_____

_____

_____

_____

_____

_____

_____

Goals Profile

1. Five years from today, how do you expect your household annual income to change?

    ❏ To grow substantially   ❏ To decrease moderately
    ❏ To grow moderately   ❏ To decrease substantially
    ❏ To stay about the same

2. What is your primary goal for your investment portfolio?

    ❏ Safety and Preservation—I don't want to ever lose money
    ❏ Safety and Income Generation—I want to take income and protect my portfolio values
    ❏ Income and Growth—I want to take income yet I still want my portfolio to grow
    ❏ Conservative Growth—I want to grow my portfolio, but I don't want significant down years
    ❏ Aggressive Growth—I want to grow my portfolio, and I'm ok having double-digit losses periodically

3. Do you expect this to change? If so, when and how?

4. Items with which you would like Estate & Financial Strategies, Inc.'s help. (Check all that apply.)

    ❏ Increase my standard of living
    ❏ Financial security at retirement
    ❏ Review the future taxation of my IRA
    ❏ Reduce my tax burden
    ❏ Simplify my financial affairs
    ❏ Review my investment portfolio
    ❏ College funding
    ❏ Provide for my family in the event of my death
    ❏ Minimize the cost of probate and estate taxes
    ❏ Control the distribution of my assets to my heirs
    ❏ Long-term care protection planning
    ❏ Other _____

5. How much income do you currently distribute from your portfolio? $_____/year.

6. Would you like more? Yes ❑ No ❑   If yes, how much income would you prefer? $_____/year.

7. Do you need (or desire) to withdraw a lump sum from your account at some point? Yes ❑ No ❑

    If yes, when? _____   And how much? _____

8. Other goals: _____

    _____

9. If you could change two things about your current financial situation what would you change?

    1) _____   2) _____

    _____   _____

Investment Goals	Low Priority									High Priority
1. Long-term growth: My return should exceed inflation rate.	1	2	3	4	5	6	7	8	9	10
2. Safety: I want my principal to be safe.	1	2	3	4	5	6	7	8	9	10
3. Current Income: I want to spend all my portfolio gains.	1	2	3	4	5	6	7	8	9	10
4. Income Taxes: I want my income taxes reduced.	1	2	3	4	5	6	7	8	9	10
5. Estate Taxes: I want my estate taxes minimized.	1	2	3	4	5	6	7	8	9	10
6. Liquidity: My principal should be immediately accessible.	1	2	3	4	5	6	7	8	9	10
7. Diversification: I want a sound asset allocation strategy.	1	2	3	4	5	6	7	8	9	10
8. Financial Advisor: I want professional management.	1	2	3	4	5	6	7	8	9	10

	Low Risk									High Risk
9. Rate your risk tolerance level.	1	2	3	4	5	6	7	8	9	10

Insurance

Life Insurance:

Insured	Company	Beneficiary	Death Benefit	Premium	Cash Value

Long-Term Care/Disability Insurance:

Insured	Company	Daily Benefit	Benefit Period	Inflation?	Premium

Property and Casualty Insurance:

What company do you use for your automobile and home insurance?

Please rank your satisfaction level (1–10 with 10 being best):

Do you have umbrella liability coverage?

If "yes," how much?

When did you last have a comprehensive review of your P&C coverages?

Income Statement

For the year beginning January 1, _____ and ending
December 31, _____.

Wages or Salary _____

   Client _____

   Spouse _____

Social Security Income _____

   Client _____

   Spouse _____

Pensions _____

   Client _____

   Spouse _____

Dividend and Interest _____

   Client _____

   Spouse _____

Capital Gains and Losses (e.g., sale of stock) _____

   Client _____

   Spouse _____

IRA, 401(k), 403(b), etc. distributions _____

   Client _____

   Spouse _____

Rents _____

Income From Business or Real Estate Sale _____

Other _____ _____

Total Annual Income: $_____

APPENDIX B

Lifestyle Expense Worksheet

Estate & Financial
Strategies, Inc.
Registered Investment Advisor

Lifestyle Expense Worksheet

Client Name _____

Household Expenses	Monthly	Annual
Rent/Lease Payment	$	$
Association Fees	$	$
Property Taxes	$	$
Property Improvements and Upkeep	$	$
Home Furnishings	$	$
Utilities		
Telephone	$	$
Cell Phone	$	$
Gas	$	$
Electric	$	$
Water/Trash	$	$
Cable TV/Satellite	$	$
Internet Service	$	$
Domestic Help	$	$
Food and Household Incidentals		
Groceries	$	$
Eating Out	$	$
Vitamins/Supplements	$	$
Household Supplies	$	$

Auto Operating and Maintenance	Monthly	Annual
Gas/Oil	$	$
Repair	$	$
Car Wash	$	$
Tags/Emissions	$	$
Parking Tolls	$	$

Personal Expenses	Monthly	Annual
Clothes and Personal Items	$	$
Personal Maintenance	$	$
Medical Expenses/Prescriptions	$	$
Laundry/Dry Cleaning	$	$
Entertainment	$	$
Hobbies	$	$
Memberships/Dues	$	$
Vacations	$	$
Books, Papers, Subscriptions	$	$
Pet Expenses	$	$
Supplies	$	$
Gifts/Birthday	$	$
Holidays	$	$
Charitable Contributions/Tithe	$	$
Alimony	$	$
Child Support	$	$
Other Court-Ordered Expenses	$	$
Other Expenses	$	$
Income Taxes	$	$
Tax Prep Fees	$	$
Attorney Fees	$	$

Insurance Premiums	Monthly	Annual
Life Insurance Premiums	$	$
Long-Term Care Premiums	$	$
Medical Insurance Premiums	$	$
Auto Insurance Premiums	$	$
House Insurance Premiums	$	$
2nd Home Insurance Premium	$	$

Loan Payments	Monthly Payment	Remaining Balance	Interest Rate	Expected Payoff Date
Mortgage Payment	$	$		
Vacation Home Payment	$	$		
Auto Loan 1 Payment	$	$		
Auto Loan 2 Payment	$	$		
RV Payment	$	$		
Boat Payment	$	$		
Loan 1 Payment	$	$		
Loan 2 Payment	$	$		
Loan 3 Payment	$	$		
Loan 4 Payment	$	$		
Other Loan Payment	$	$		

Goals and Dreams	Monthly Amount	Annual Amount	Up-Front Cost	Expected Date of Purchase
Goal 1	$	$		
Goal 2	$	$		
Goal 3	$	$		
Goal 4	$	$		
Goal 5	$	$		
Goal 6	$	$		

APPENDIX C

Financial Lifestyle Fact Finder

Financial Lifestyle Fact Finder

Personal Information

Client Name _____

Spouse Name _____

Home Address _____

City, State, Zip _____

Home Ph _____ Hus Cell Ph _____ Wife Cell Ph _____

E-mail address: _____

Years at Current Address _____

Client DL # _____ Spouse DL # _____

Client Birthdate _____ SSN _____

Client Birthdate _____ SSN _____

Client's Employer _____ Client's Work Ph _____

Position/Duties _____ Yrs at Current Employer _____

Spouse's Employer _____ Spouse's Work ph _____

Spouse's Position/Duties _____

Spouse's Yrs at Current Employer _____

Do you have an Attorney? _____ Name? _____

Do you have an Accountant? _____ Name? _____

Do you expect to care for a child or parent? _____

Do you have a financial adviser? _____

Any problems with previous stockbrokers? _____

Children	Address	Social Security #	Date of Birth

Grandchildren	Parent	Date of Birth

General

Briefly explain your concerns and how you feel we may be able to help you:

_____

_____

_____

_____

Protection

	Yes	No	Uncertain
Do you have any potential health problems?	___	___	_____
Have you ever been declined or rated for insurance?	___	___	_____
Have you smoked in the last two years?	___	___	_____

Concerns:

_____

_____

_____

Retirement Planning

At what age would you like to retire? _____

Annual before-tax income desired in today's dollars $ _____

Are you covered by any company retirement plans? _____

If so, what is the amount of your expected monthly $ _____
benefits?

Are you expecting a distribution from your retirement _____
plan soon?

Concerns:

_____

_____

_____

Financial Planning

	No Concern					Very Concerned				
Planning for children and grandchildren	1	2	3	4	5	6	7	8	9	10
Reducing current income taxes	1	2	3	4	5	6	7	8	9	10
Increasing current income	1	2	3	4	5	6	7	8	9	10
Estate planning	1	2	3	4	5	6	7	8	9	10
Desire for professional management	1	2	3	4	5	6	7	8	9	10
Maximum growth	1	2	3	4	5	6	7	8	9	10
Combined growth and income	1	2	3	4	5	6	7	8	9	10

Estate Planning

	Yes	No	Uncertain
1. Do you have an updated/adequate will?	___	___	_____
2. Do you have a General Durable Power of Attorney (POA)?	___	___	_____

3. Do you have a POA for health care? ___ ___ _____

4. Have you established any trusts? ___ ___ _____

5. Are you the beneficiary of any trusts? ___ ___ _____

6. Are you expecting a significant inheritance? ___ ___ _____

7. If so, how much and when? _____

8. Have you developed an asset protection strategy to protect your assets from civil litigation? _____

9. Amount of capital you would like to preserve in your estate for your survivors:

   $ _____ or _____% of your final estate value

Concerns:

_____

_____

_____

_____

_____

Conscious Investor Quiz

Yes   No

___ ___   1. Do you have a customized game plan to guide your lifelong investment decisions?

___ ___   2. Have you established a written agreement that outlines expectations for your relationship with your financial professional?

___ ___   3. Have you determined a method for measuring the success of your portfolio?

___ ___   4. Have you deliberately assessed the gap between where you are right now and where you want to be five years from now?

___ ___   5. Do you understand the role of diversification in a successful investment portfolio?

___ ___   6. Do you know how to measure risk in your portfolio?

___ ___   7. Can you identify the cultural messages that shape your view of money?

___ ___   8. Have you identified your investment philosophy?

___ ___   9. Do you understand how "the market" really works?

___ ___   10. Have you identified your needed rate of return from your portfolio?

Investment

Investment Objective (please check one)

1. Preserving existing assets above all else   _____

2. Preserving existing assets combined with growth
    for inflation   _____

3. Conservative income with minimum risk   _____

4. Maximum income with some risk   _____

5. Conservative growth of asset, income secondary,
    some risk   _____

6. Maximum growth of assets, substantial risk   _____

7. Are there any investments you are opposed to or have had a
    bad experience with and, if so, what are they?

_____

_____

Concerns:

_____

_____

Income

Employment Income	Client	Spouse	Total
Salary, Wages			
Business Income			

Taxable Investment	Client	Spouse	Total
Interest			
Dividend			
Rents, Partnerships			
Other			

Miscellaneous Income	Client	Spouse	Total
Pension			
Social Security			
Other			

Assets

Checking, Savings, Money Market, CDs, and Cash

Bank or Company	Account Type	Balance	Interest Rate	Term

Mutual Funds

Description	Number of Shares	Market Value	Original Cost	Cost Basis

Stocks/Bonds

Description	His/Her/Joint	Market Value	Original Cost Basis

Annuities

Company	Origin Date	Premium	Account Value	Surrender Value	Cost Basis

Company Retirement Plans and IRAs

Company	Account Value	Interest

Partnerships

Description	Type	Units	Value	Owner

Real Estate

Description	Market Value	Cost	Date Acquired

Liabilities

Owed to	Current Balance	Original Amount	Loan Term	Interest Rate

Insurance

Life Insurance

Company	Origin Date	Cash Value	Owner/Insured	Face Value

Disability Insurance

Company	Origin Date	Account Value	Owner/Insured	Premium

Long-Term Care Insurance

Company	Insured	Benefit	Premium

Umbrella Policy

Company	Insured	Benefit	Premium

Acknowledgments

A big thank you to the following people for their invaluable help. You have my sincerest and most heartfelt appreciation:

To Mark Victor Hansen for this coaching, his encouragement, and for introducing me to the right people at the right time; you were the catalyst for taking me from the *idea* of writing this book to the *reality* of writing this book.

To Debra Englander for her interest in my book, her patience, and her perseverance in working with me and opening the door to all the tremendous resources at Wiley. To Emilie Herman for her insightful edits in making this a better book. To Stacey Fischkelta for helping me stay on task, not always the easiest thing to do. To Adrianna Johnson for her capable assistance. To the design team for creating the imaginative book cover design.

To Ed Slott and his team for their personal mission of teaching and training advisers in the intricacies and complexities of IRAs and retirement plans to better serve their clients. A personal thank you for inviting me to participate in your vision and for your invaluable advice over the years. A special thank you to IRA Technical Consultant, Beverly Deveny, for her review and greatly appreciated input on the IRA Master Chapter.

To Henry Abts and his company The Estate Plan, especially to Geri McHam. Thank you for your review and insights on the Estate

Planning chapter. Your personal support and encouragement meant a great deal to me. I regret not finishing the book before Henry's passing; his legacy and mission lives on through his family, his company, and the wonderful team there.

To Mark Matson of Matson Money in Mason, OH, who first introduced me to the Fama/French Investment models and opened my eyes to the truths about money and investing. Whether it has been through sharing the story of investing, separating the myths from the truths, or his continual personal coaching and insights, I owe Mark a debt of gratitude for advancing my education, thus making me a better adviser to my clients.

To Larry Swedroe, Principal and Director of Research for The Buckingham Family of Financial Services, for his "tweaking" of the Introduction and Investment chapter. In the process of writing his eleventh book, I am truly thankful for his suggestions as an author and very knowledgeable investment adviser.

To Jack Marrion for your review of Chapter 4 and your excellent research on FIAs. I look forward to each issue of your newsletter, *The Index Compendium,* a great resource for unbiased scientific research, statistics, and accurate information on Index Annuities.

To Sheryl J. Moore, President and CEO of Advantage Group Associates, Inc., for her review and input on Chapter 4. Sheryl is an acknowledged, sought after, and oft quoted expert independent market research analyst. Her web sites are an excellent resource for factual information on annuities and index life insurance: www .sheryljmoore.com.

To Russ Cook, Board Certified Estate Planning Attorney, co-host of the Retirement Report, and trusted colleague. Thank you for your corrections to the probate flow chart and help with the Estate Planning chapter.

A big thank you to my friend and colleague Friday Burke, Ph.D., EA, host of the *Dr. Friday* radio show, and my co-host on the *Retirement Report,* for her insights and input on planning for small business owners.

To Bill Mullen and Jim VonBruchhaeuser, for their review and knowledgeable contributions on the Long-Term Care chapter.

To Anthony and Denise Cloutier (The Cloutier Group's Estate & Financial Strategies in Ossipee, NH), my business partners and collaborators in the creation of the curriculum and workbook for the accompanying educational courses to the book. Their teaching backgrounds coupled with their commitment to the business practices outlined in this book make them unique and valued advisers to me and their clients (www.cloutiergroupefs.com).

To the following trusted advisers who opened up their very successful organizations to me and were so generous with their time in sharing their best practices, principles, and values in building their businesses and serving their clients. They have been instrumental in the development of my business and the creation of the systems and strategies described in this book:

Chip Hollingsworth, CRP, ChFEBC, Federal Employee Benefits Assistance Agency (F.E.B.A.A.), Albertville, AL (http://fedfriends .com).

George Wells, Legacy of America, Auburn Hills, MI (www .legacyofamerica.com).

Mark Lloyd, RFC, Blake Morris, CFP, M.B.A ., and Drew Jones, B.B.A., The Lloyd Group, Suwanee, GA (http://www .thelloydgroupinc.com)

Benjie Lloyd, Senior Strategies, Inc., Pelham, AL, (www .seniorstrategies.cc).

Samuel J. Liang and Richard L. Rubino, JD, Rubino & Liang, LLC, Newton, MA (www.rubinoandliang.com) A special thank you to their right-hand-man, John Conley, for all of his time and assistance.

Michael J. Hainer, Hainer & Berman, P.C., Bingham Farms, MI (www.hainerberman.com).

Patrick M. Simasko, JD, Simasko, Simasko & Simasko, P.C., Mount Clemens, MI, (www.simaskolaw.com).

Dan White, Founder and President, CLU, ChFC, Daniel A. White & Associates, Glen Mills, PA, (www.danwhiteandassociates.com).

Thank you to everyone at M&O Marketing for your help with this book and my business. Your commitment over the years in helping me find solutions for my clients allows me to better serve them.

Most importantly to Dennis Brown, the first to plant the idea of writing this book in me and whose unflagging support and encouragement have been instrumental in bringing it into being. I have always been able to count on you as one of my most trusted mentors, advisers, and friends in business and in my personal life.

Equally to Tim Otto, "the silent partner." Your support behind the scenes does not go unnoticed. Not only do I respect your integrity and business acumen, but I also appreciate and value your friendship.

More than just valued business associates, your willingness to go the extra mile sets you apart from any organization that I have ever worked with. You exemplify the same principles and values that guide me in my business and my life: LeeAnn Xuereb, Dawn Cwik, Nancy Collins, Nancy Turnquist, Kathy Spaw, Stephanie Murphy, Jessica Robbins, Ryan Kus, Kim Ricketts, Heather Cobb, Jason Oberst, Kim Yaldoo, Nicole Fisher, Charlotte Bewersdorff, and Darcy Smith.

I give full credit for the good and take full responsibility for the bad.

About the Author

Hank Parrott, ChFC, AEP, is President of Estate & Financial Strategies, Inc., a registered investment advisory firm located in Brentwood, Tennessee. The firm's mission is to serve as his clients' "Personal CFO," assisting them in achieving the goals and objectives that are most important to them by integrating all areas of planning including financial, insurance, tax, and legal strategies.

Mr. Parrott holds more than a dozen licenses and designations and continues to improve his knowledge base by attending several advance planning industry meetings held throughout the year. He has been featured on numerous television and radio programs, including *In Your Prime, Retirement Living,* CNBC's *Morning Call,* and is the host of *Retirement Report* and the *Financial Lifestyle Show.* Each year, Mr. Parrott educates area investors by holding educational seminars open to the public on topics ranging from taking money out of IRAs tax-free, avoiding unfair taxes on Social Security income, how to get long-term care protection without paying annual premiums, safe investment alternatives, protecting yourself from market losses, and much more.

Hank and his wife, Pat, live in Franklin, Tennessee, where they enjoy spending time with their two daughters, Hannah and Laurel.

Index